Morocco and the Sahara

Morocco and the Sahara

Social Bonds and Geopolitical Issues

Mohamed Cherkaoui

The Bardwell Press, Oxford

Published by:

The Bardwell Press
6 Bardwell Road
Oxford OX2 6SW
www.bardwell-press.co.uk

British Library Cataloguing in Publication Data
A catalogue record for this book is available from the British Library

ISBN-13: 978-1-905622-03-0

Typeset by The Bardwell Press, Oxford, UK
Printed in Great Britain by TJ International, Padstow, Cornwall

Contents

PREFACE   *ix*

INTRODUCTION
   To Erase History is to Mortgage the Future   *1*

PART ONE: Stratocracy or Democracy?

CHAPTER 1
   Balance of Power in the Maghreb: Impact on the
   Geostrategic Future of the Greater Middle East   *9*
      1/ Unending Blackmail   10
      2/ The Imperial *Hubris*   13
      3/ A Theory of the Imperial Temptation: On Stratocracy   20
      4/ Strategic Consequences: *Pax Algeriana*   27

CHAPTER 2
   The State in Crisis: On Tribal Temptation and the
   De-territorialization of Terrorism   *39*
      1/ Crisis of the State, American and French Initiatives   40
      2/ Temptation of Tribalism and Danger of Relativism   46

CHAPTER 3
   Morocco and its "Silent Revolution"   *51*
      1/ Reforms   52
      2/ Autonomy of the Sahara and Its Institutional Foundations   55

PART TWO: Social and Economic Integration of the Western Sahara

CHAPTER 4

Integration and its Measurement   *69*

1/ Fields of Study   71
2/ Dimensions, Indicators and Measurement of the Concept of
   Integration   72
3/ Available Statistics, Data to be Constructed and Problems
   of Method   77

CHAPTER 5

Declining Illiteracy   *81*

1/ Falling Trends in Illiteracy   82
2/ Comparison Between the Saharan and Non Saharan Regions   84
3/ Relationship Between Illiteracy and Socio-economic Variables   86
Principal Conclusions   93
Appendix to Chapter 5   95

CHAPTER 6

Substantial and Rapid Increase in School Enrolment in the
Sahara   *101*

1/ Evolution of School Enrolment   102
2/ Testing the Hypotheses of the Influence of Educational Policy   109
3/ Generalization of these Results to the Saharan Provinces   115
Conclusion   117
Appendix to Chapter 6   119

CHAPTER 7

Human and Social Development   *123*

1/ Poverty Index of the Saharan Regions   123
2/ Evolution of Poverty and Regional Comparisons   132

CHAPTER 8

Marriage in the Sahara   *137*

1/ The Study: Data and Limitations   138
2/ Change in Regional Endogamy Rates and its Meaning   142
3/ Trends in Marital Exchange by Social Milieu   149
Conclusion   152
Appendix to Chapter 8   153

CHAPTER 9

Modernization Processes and Social Movements   *159*

1/ Economic Integration of the Sahara and Modernization
   Indicators   161
2/ Modernization and Social Movements   169

CONTENTS

CONCLUSION   177

APPENDIX OF MAPS   181

BIBLIOGRAPHY   189

INDEX   197

Preface

This essay has come about in response to a pressing question on the Sahara from a friend of mine. He knows quite well that the Maghreb does not fall within the scope of my research topics. Cultural area sociological studies have never enjoyed a special status within the stratified world of scientific research and, except in a few instances, it is something more often associated with demanding journalism than fundamental research seeking a solution to sociological puzzles by combining theories and empirical data rather than the pure narration of accumulated facts.

No matter how hard I explained to him that the issue was very complex and that it was loaded with so much emotion that I might be accused of bias, he stuck to his guns and reminded me of our previous discussions on relations in the Maghreb. Facing such huge insistence and tenacity and the immense but, I will admit, intellectually stimulating difficulties, I accepted the challenge of writing an essay on an issue which poisons the life of several peoples and which might prevent them from ever seeing the creation of the Maghreb they hope for.

During this journey, my reading of the works of anthropologists, historians, lawmakers, sociologists and strategists was undoubtedly an enriching phase. I do not claim to have covered all the areas of knowledge that a demanding expert is supposed to be in command of. I am aware of my deficiencies. The interviews that I had with several colleagues and eminent politicians were a source of pleasure for me. The most difficult and extenuating stage was obviously that of data collection. Actually, I was seeking to test assumptions rather than engage in literary narration.

The problem of the Sahara revolves in fact around three main axes. The first axis concerns historical and legal legitimacy. It is well-documented. The historians of the French and Spanish colonization of North Africa came up with highly scientific publications. They accurately dated, depicted and analysed the stages of colonization from the second quarter of the nineteenth century up to the independence of the countries of the region. In this secular historical process, huge Moroccan territories had been, through force, annexed to French Algeria, many populations had been displaced by force, the rest of Morocco had been shared by France in the centre and Spain in the North and South under agreements dating back to 1904 and 1911 between the two colonizing powers. These are facts that hardly anyone can argue against even if the masters of independent Algeria have relentlessly sought to protect the heritage that colonial France handed over to them by breaking their word, by denying history and by calling for the principle of inviolability of the borders inherited from the colonisers.

That is the second axis. The problem of the Sahara will always remain obscure and even incomprehensible if one refuses to take into account the serious territorial dispute between Morocco and Algeria, and what I call the imperial *hubris* of the masters of Algiers. I put forward a tentative explanation for this here. It runs counter to some theories of imperialism that support the thesis of the end of nation-state sovereignty and the emergence of a unique imperial global power. These theories do not attach much importance to the attempts made to create great regional powers. They forget that, like other types of phenomena, international relations are stratified and located in several levels of reality that correspond to different organizational levels.

The third axis is sociological. It concerns the issue of the social bond between the Sahrawis and the rest of the Moroccan population. It has never been dealt with as systematically and rigorously as it deserves. I devote the bulk of the analyses of the chapters in this essay to it. I attempt to test the hypothesis that these bonds do exist, that they are not just historically established but that they form today a social fabric of such homogeneity, density, and power that can hardly be ignored in any final settlement of the Sahara problem. I am not favouring one indicator of social bonds to buttress a *pro domo* plea; I am looking for them all as long as empirical data are available. Still better, I have even designed some to address a daring and risky challenge: I intend to analyse all the 'Adoulian' registers of marriage contracts over four decades to test the hypothesis that heterogamous marriage between the Sahrawis and the rest of the Moroccan population has gradually risen to such an extent that it would be impossible for a politically right and morally irreproachable Solomon to separate families into two radically heterogeneous entities. I could add that the demonstration might have been perfect had I possessed marriage contracts of the Sahrawis living in other areas of Morocco than in the Sahara. Within this population, the rate of heterogamous marriage is undoubtedly higher. This can easily accounted for by basic social mechanisms. Collecting this information is beyond the modest resources I have available and would have taken a vast amount of time. Who would venture into scrutinizing thousands of registers lying on the shelves of archive rooms of local courts throughout the kingdom without having to recruit an armada of investigators.

I should also admit to not being able to construct statistics pertaining to the private investments of the Sahrawis and non-Sahrawis in the Sahara and in other Moroccan regions to test the hypothesis of economic integration that I can subject however to other analyses and empirical tests. Such an endeavour would have taken too much time and a team of investigators would have had to compile a set of documents scattered nationwide. The non-systematic information that some people were kind enough to share with me pleads in favour of the general thesis put forward here. I do not rely upon it for understandable reasons: there is no guarantee that this is a representative sample.

I benefited from the support of many people in this venture. I cannot cite them all. I am particularly indebted to his Excellency Mohamed Cherkaoui, an exceptional personality with capable of profound and cogent analyses, possessed of vast learning in Arab and Western cultures, and a perfect knowledge of people and the world supported by an extraordinary memory that the reader would hardly believe possible, that make him an indispensable authority. I am also grateful to his Excellency Ahmed Lahlimi Alami, High Commissioner for Planning, who was kind enough to put all the census data and all the studies undertaken by his department at my disposal. How could I dare to forget to thank all those enthusiastic people working in the shade who agreed to come along on this arduous trip? I am thinking here of those who have done their utmost to enlighten me on the issues and border disputes between Morocco and Algeria that they know so well after having worked on them for at least half a century. I am also concerned to thank those who have helped me understand the nuts and bolts of their cameral science. Last but not least, my thanks to all those who extended their valuable assistance by collecting data or scrutinizing the manuscript registers of marriage contracts in accordance with the research plan I provided to them.

At the threshold of this work, and before he or she embarks upon it, I would like the reader to understand that while I do not have the slightest doubt about the common fate of these people living under the same sky in the southern shore of the Mediterranean at the Northern borders of Mauritania, I have, however, complied with what any researcher considers to be at the core of his/her calling, namely a search for the truth. To this effect, I monitored all the statistics used by cross checking. I used all of them, those that support the central thesis as well as those that weaken it. I have not sought to conceal employment crises or the social or political movements in the Sahara and elsewhere, nor have been indulgent towards the administration or certain social networks. I request the reader's forgiveness if I have been mistaken. That was certainly not intentional.

Introduction

To Erase History is to Mortgage the Future

To our very gracious servants, the caïds of the tribes of Ihamed of Touat, to their cadhis, to their Chorfa—may God protect them—to their Merabitines and to all their very important persons,— ... We have come to learn about what had happened at Ain-Salah, the arrival of some people from the Algerian Province, their violent intrusion among the inhabitants, their aggression against the state of peace, the treaties and conventions between the two governments, with no respect for what has mutually been agreed upon in the regulations pertaining to border demarcation, with no possible justification even by flow or back flow, since the people in the region advised them of their being the subjects of Our Person elevated by God, and being part of Our fortunate empire ...

Such is the message quoted by Captain Martin (1923) that the King of Morocco, Moulay Abdelaziz, had sent on March 15 1900 to the inhabitants of Touat, his subjects. The French column arrived at Ain Salah on March 14 equipped with one thousand rifles, two cannons and one hundred and fifty swords. Stout-hearted but inadequately armed to defend themselves, the Moroccans in the oases paid dearly for their resistance with 500 to 600 casualties and many prisoners. The French expedition ended with 11 French casualties and 44 injured. One year prior to the massacre, the *Tricouleur* was already hanging over the oases of Tidikelt despite the armed resistance of the population who vainly informed the invaders that the region was part of the Cherifian domain. The vast Moroccan Saharan region was subjected and annexed to French Algeria.

One can read in the same book, through the official mail between the leading figures of these regions, the representatives of the authorities and the king himself, the vicissitudes of French colonization of these Saharan territories that were part of what was called the Cherifian Empire. One would also find there letters exchanged between the kings of Morocco and their Saharan subjects, testimonies to the political bond between the tribes of that large region and the Moroccan kings from at least the beginning of the 16th century, the four centuries that Martin's book covers. In fact the French gunboat had come to annihilate nine centuries of political bonds.

The same goes for both Western Sahara and Eastern Sahara. The number of official documents testifying to the allegiances bonding the inhabitants of these Saharan regions to the king of Morocco is sizable and persuasive. It suffices only to open Martin's publications in particular, as well as the five volumes published by The Hague International Court of Justice (1979–82) to get the point.

Let us look into one of them. In 1884, when the Spaniards occupied for the first time a point in the Atlantic coast of Western Sahara, the ambassador of the Spanish king enquired a few months later about the southern borders of the Cherifian Empire. In his response dated June 1886, Moulay Hassan, King of Morocco, specified that Oued Ed-Dahab, le Rio de Oro, was part of his kingdom and the inhabitants therein were his subjects in compliance with the norms of Muslim law, the only valid law that set obligations on both parties.

The colonization of the Western Sahara by Spain was very slow and difficult particularly because of the resistance of Ma El Ainain who, armed and funded by the King of Morocco, called for war to be waged against the colonisers from Smara. Other resistance movements and other uprisings followed and slowed down the progress of the Spanish colonisers. The map (A2, pp. 182–183) representing the different stages of the Spanish occupation between 1884 and 1937 is self-explanatory in this regard.

In June 1900, an agreement was signed between France and Spain, circumscribing and separating the French possessions that made up

Mauritania and the future Spanish Sahara. Another French-Spanish agreement was signed later in 1904. It remained confidential until 1912, date of the setting up of the French protectorate over Morocco. It allowed for the splitting of Morocco in two zones of influence, one French zone to the south and another Spanish one to the north. Ifni and Sakia El Hamra regions were handed over to Spain, which was experiencing great difficulty in imposing its rule upon them.

But, beyond the issue of the legitimacy of the political bond between Sahara and Morocco, the economy and the society, and even the livelihood of this Saharan population was only viable thanks to the hinterland of Tekna and their relations with the vast region stretching from Sous up to Marrakech and even beyond. Naïmi's studies, especially the latest (Naïmi 2004), provide ample evidence to that effect. Compared to those of the populations of the other Moroccan regions, the history, culture and religious practices of the Sahrawis seem more rooted in this arabo-berber Moorish civilization, specific to Morocco since the Almoravids, the Saharan Berbers of the large Sanhadja group, who controlled North Africa in the second half of the 11th and all 12th centuries. All the other dynasties that came afterwards, from the Almohads to the Alaouis, took over this heritage and strengthened it. Without the Sahara, Morocco's history would be incomprehensible, and without Morocco, Sahara would be no more than desert.

One might certainly attempt to erase history for partisan reasons; it cannot, however, be contested. Some seem to suffer from an amazing collective amnesia; but by the same token they mortgage their future.

This essay does not attempt to rewrite the history of the bonds between Morocco and Western Sahara. Others more skilled than I have undertaken this endeavour. My essay has other ambitions. It sets the issue of Sahara in its regional and international context and sheds thereby some light on the strategies of the masters of Algiers. Their desire for power, this imperial *hubris* that haunts them and of which they have become prisoners, takes them away from the new realities of their country, of the region and of the world. Should we then keep reminding them that Sahara has never been a problem for the Algerian people? They should venture out of their conclave to heed the *vox populi*.

This essay also draws attention to the perverse geopolitical effects that the balkanization of the region might generate. It presents the hypothesis that the problems of terrorism, of the massive migrations threatening all of Europe, are unlikely be solved through the billions of dollars poured into the desert sand and the Maghreb or through the logistic support that the region has been getting since September 11, 2001.

It also seeks to place the solution to the autonomy of the Saharan regions in the framework of the major reforms already under way, the silent revolution that Morocco triggered ten years ago and that opens new political perspectives to the other regions in the kingdom and to the neighbouring countries to engage along the path of confederal democracy rather than that of stratocracy. The reader should not be mistaken about it: I am aware that there is a long way to go and of the burdensome heritage that has already been analysed and accounted for. I refer in particular to the testimony of the historian Abdallah Laroui. But for god's sake, let us stop the attacks waged against the first flowers of a democratic spring in Morocco on the grounds that the other Arab regimes from the Atlantic shore to the Red Sea are so authoritarian that they are not even worthy of criticism. Remonstrances are, for sure, beneficial provided they are measured and fair.

This sociological study raises questions, at last and above all, about the integration of the Sahrawi populations, and in a more general manner about this mixture of tribes, men and women as different from each other as the regions that have decided to share a common fate and a common Morocco with its distinctive history.

This political, economic and social integration is, in my view, the most essential element for the present and the future. I will try to depict its evolution, and also explain it by identifying its major determinants. I will certainly take time to analyse the economic and sociological data of the last four decades to really get a clear picture of its reality and scope. What better argument can be put forth than that of the matrimonial exchange between the Sahrawis and the other Moroccans? One can always set barriers and artificial borders, but one cannot annihilate the desire of living together with others, which can be expressed in ways other than through referendum.

In this century where new economic and political clusters are being created, where people are becoming aware of their common fate and understanding the necessity for a democratic federalism, we are witnessing false dissensions in the Maghreb. Whatever the solution is these problems, the peoples of this Mediterranean region are predestined to union on pain of being relegated to the margin of history and of never being able to take part in the forceful march of global civilisations. What Maghrebian country would claim to be able to single-handedly meet the challenge of fierce but beneficial international competition in the economic, cultural, scientific and technical spheres? Who would boast they were able alone to achieve this critical mass without which no efficient action could be undertaken? Who would boast to have enough clout to guarantee the survival of its people, give them work, and ensure the future of their children? The modest dimensions of the countries of the region cannot allow even for the emergence of effective educational systems, and world-standard universities. If we examine the last 2006 world universities assessment by the Institute of Higher Education of Shanghai Jiao Tong University, not one single North African or Arab country has a university that ranks among the 500 top universities, apart from that modest 404th rank of Cairo University.

Nonetheless, the Maghreb contains many Schumpeterian entrepreneurs, a bright intelligentsia, particularly Algerian, which is highly present and visible through its publications in the major international scientific journals. Its members are found at the highest levels in the best European and American universities and research centres. Yet it has been cruelly lacking in its native country. But, who would dare to put the onus on it? The mind can only breathe when it is free.

Pierre-André Coffinhal, president of the Revolutionary Tribunal when the case of the unfortunate Lavoisier was before him, told the scientist—who had asked for some time to finish his chemistry experiments before being taken to the guillotine—that the Revolution was not in need of scientists. The only thing history records from this obscure judge is his sad retort. But humanity carries on celebrating the memory of the great scientist, rather than political terror.

Part One

Stratocracy or Democracy?

1

Balance of Power in the Maghreb

Impact on the Geostrategic Future of the Greater
Middle East

"A new distemper has spread itself over Europe, infecting our princes,
and inducing them to keep up an exorbitant number of troops. It has
its redoublings, and of necessity becomes contagious. For as soon as
one prince augments his forces, the rest of course do the same; so that
nothing is gained thereby but the public ruin." I am not suggesting
that the validity of this theory of the balance of power, so admirably
presented in Montesquieu's *Spirit of Laws,* is entirely unconditional;
however, it is still applicable to many geostrategic configurations.[1] Such
is the case in the Maghreb. Any massive rearming of a regional power
irrevocably alters the balance of power, re-established only at the cost
of an equivalent effort on the part of the opposite side and close to the
critical threshold beyond which war has every chance of breaking out.
The history of international relations is full of lessons to be learned, and
those who do not remember the past are condemned to repeat it.

Since the time of Thucydides, the arms race has proven to be a
process of mechanical self-stimulation. The Greek historian used it to
explain the Peloponnesian wars.[2] It condemns the players to a non-
cooperative non-zero-sum game, the most famous example of which
is the dreadful game of the prisoner's dilemma, well known for its

perverse effects. One does not have to be a great scholar to understand that in a structure of the prisoner's dilemma, the only rational strategy the relevant parties can adopt, if they do not want to embark on the road to ruin, is a policy of non-cooperation even if it proves to be more costly than cooperation.[3] The United States and the former Soviet Union played that game for half a century. Without the master stroke of President Reagan which, by initiating the Strategic Defense Initiative, led both superpowers to astronomic expenditures that were ruinous for the Soviet Union and contributed to the collapse of the Soviet Empire, we would still be today in the throes of the cold war.[4]

1/ UNENDING BLACKMAIL

One must fear that the same phenomenon could occur between Algeria and Morocco. The recent massive rearmament of Algeria, in particular with the help of Russia, the total cost of which amounts to several billion dollars, risks provoking a dangerous spiral the consequences of which no one can predict or tell how long it will last. But no one is being fooled. What is presented as a modernization of the Algerian army is nothing more than a pretext. It entails heavy armaments that observers interpret as a clear-cut message sent to Algeria's neighbours with regard to the considerable financial power this nation has and to the determination of Algerian leaders that some people will clearly see as a threat, or at least as a dissuasive build-up. Confronted by this challenge, Morocco is forced to use the strategy of non-cooperation; if not, it will risk the infliction of fatal and irreversible harm. Therefore, one can understand why Morocco seeks to strengthen its defense capabilities.

This is not the place to speculate on the Algerian nuclear program, on the suspicion and fear that it generates among its most immediate neighbours, as well as in the United States and southern Europe. Even if no irrefutable proof exists, for the time being, of Algeria's intentions to obtain nuclear weapons, a series of disturbing indications have led international experts to ask serious questions. To mention all of them would not be appropriate here. Yet we can cite some of the most topical ones so as to give them serious consideration.

1/ The scale of the second "Es Salam" nuclear reactor of Ain Oussara, constructed with assistance from China, and the high level of anti-missile air defences with which it is equipped;

2/ The potentialities it will eventually offer for producing nuclear arms the dangers of which lead one of the most eminent American non-proliferation specialists to call for shut down;

3/ The outcomes of analyses made by certain Western services, in particular Spain and the United States, on the Algerian nuclear program;

4/ The conclusions of the military in certain high commands and institutes of strategic studies, especially in France;

5/ The visit in late November 2006 of General Jing Zhiyuan, the chief of China's strategic military force, and his meeting with Guenaïza Abdelmalek, Deputy Minister of the Ministry of Defense, and the chief of the general headquarters of the National Army of Liberation, General Ahmed Gaïd Salah;

6/ The countless visits to Algiers of Iranian military figures, and those by former President Khatami accompanied by the Vice-Minister of Defense, Hassan Rouhani, in charge of Iranian security and of the nuclear program, by Admiral Ali Chemkhani, Ali Larijani, Supreme Secretary of the National Iranian Security Council and chief negotiator of the Iranian nuclear program;

7/ The multiple offers of advice and help by Iran to Algeria on nuclear matters.

All these factors constitute a series of largely negative indices. They raise uncertainties in the minds of many observers concerning the real intentions of the Algerian authorities.

It is true that Algeria signed the Non-Proliferation Treaty on nuclear weapons. But in spite of the insistence of the highest international authorities, we still await Algeria's adherence to the additional protocol giving increased control to the International Atomic Energy Agency, enabling it to carry out unscheduled and unannounced visits to the facilities of the signatory countries. Algeria is among those countries that do not have nuclear weapons, but potentially the most ready to try to acquire some, just like Argentina, Brazil, Syria, Belarus, and Egypt. Numerous strategic studies point this out.

It is likely that the argument put forth by the Algerian authorities, according to which it would be unjust and unfair to apply the policy of double standards—a reference to India and Israel—is only a false issue hiding a long-term vision. It is important to note that Algeria is not a signatory to the Missile Technology Control Regime. This grouping of countries, let us recall, seeks to impede the proliferation of vectors of uncontrolled proliferatio⌐ ⌐ of weapons of mass destruction.

Undoubtedly, because the country has faced a general outcry by international opinion against its nuclear ambitions, and the reckless attempts by Algiers to move ahead with its illegal projects for the building of weapons of mass destruction, the Algerian authorities have stopped their programme. Not only are we not totally reassured, but popular wisdom has it that he/she who once dared begin, can always decide to continue. Suspicion is thus created and grievances boosted. Cato, who was afraid that the second Punic war would be forgotten along with the terror it engendered, wound up all his speeches with the famous epimone, *delenda est carthago* (Carthage must be destroyed). Obviously, historical parallels are risky but there is nothing to prevent us from drawing lessons from them.

Consideration should be given to the Iranian case. The great powers should take a second look at it before issuing assuaging declarations pursuant to the purely peaceful use of any nuclear program, Algerian or otherwise. In this sphere, the separation between civilian and military power is, to say the least, unclear. Benevolent neutrality and appeasing attitudes can no longer serve as the foundation of a responsible international policy.

One can understand why a country like India, which has no fossil energy resources, and which is counting on the construction of pipelines stretching from the Near East to the Indian sub-continent, crossing through areas of great instability, would need to develop civilian uses of its nuclear program. But we might not think the same of Iran, the fourth ranking world oil producer exporting three quarters of its output. It is even harder to understand this in the case of Algeria, the oil output of which is entirely exported, and slated to cover 40% of European demand for gas, and in the near future to export electricity to that continent.

There is good reason for concern when the Iranian president is heard to declare that his country is ready to share expertise in nuclear energy with Algeria. Since there has been little determined reaction against the Iranian model of behaviour, one might rightly expect the same attitude from potential imitators. Perhaps we will be saying goodbye to non-proliferation with Algeria, Saudi Arabia heading the Gulf Cooperation Council, Egypt, Syria and Turkey certain to follow the Iranian example.

Algeria, even more than Iran, is so huge that it would be easy to conceal any enrichment centrifuges, making their destruction impossible, in accordance with the scenario developed by Iran. Colossal resources would be required to search the "belly of the earth" for hidden units across a territory of nearly 2,400,000 km^2, i.e. one and a half times greater than Iran.

2/ THE IMPERIAL *HUBRIS*

In fact this is only one of the manifestations that we can depict here as integral to the Algerian imperial *hubris*. This exaggerated pride, this all-encompassing passion and desire to inflict shame on others, has been identified in other contexts, firstly by the Babylonian Sumerians, by Hesiod, and later by philosophers and ancient Greek tragedians. Mesopotamian and Hellenistic ethos considered it as the ultimate evil. Both disorder and misfortune are intimately linked to this form of anomie.[5]

Independent Algeria has not only practised the expansionist policy of colonial France but has actually extended it and draped it with the red flag of the revolution. The pupil has gone further than the teacher. Let me explain more clearly: when I refer to Algeria, I am not talking about the people, but rather its leaders who are the expression of a total ideology, the architects of an imperial policy, rationally and methodically devised and implemented. Therefore, in this word and its correlates are nothing more than condensed forms of well-thought out realities at the individual and institutional level.

Unfortunately, space prevents me from recounting the history of the progressive expansion of Algeria to the detriment of neighbouring countries, principally Morocco. The historians of colonization have described this in great detail.

One overriding fact deserves calm reflection. On the eve of French colonization in 1830, the coastal strip under the former Turkish administration extended no further than the 32nd parallel and was a part of the Ottoman Empire, later unified by the French army and called "Algeria", with a territory of no more than 300,000 km^2. Officially, in 1920, the total surface area of French Algeria was 575,000 km^2. At the time of independence in 1962, it was nearly 2,400,000 km^2!

An explanation of this historical miracle is quite simple. Along with its conquest, France also attached to Algeria, which in those days was a French Department, the major part of French Saharan Africa.

Therefore, one cannot be surprised that an annexation of this scale gives rise to border disputes that are hard to accept by the states considering themselves to have lost a part of their territory. We know most about those between Algeria and its two neighbours, Tunisia and Morocco.

The borders of Algeria were disputed by Tunisia at the end of the Protectorate in 1956. Tunisia claimed the strip below and above the 32nd parallel made up by the rectangle defined by the summits of Bir Romane to the northwest, Fort Saint Louis to the southwest, Bir Aioun to the northeast and Tiarat to the southeast.

While it was conducting a war of independence, the Algerian National Liberation Front (FLN), fearing partition by the Joint Organization of Saharan Regions, suggested recognition of its sovereignty over the entire Sahara and that, once it was independent, Algeria would be ready to settle border disputes and cooperate to jointly develop existing resources. President Bourguiba accepted the principle of this following the agreement signed between His Majesty Hassan II and President Ferhat Abbas. The Algerians took the same line with both the Tunisians and Moroccans.

Once independence was proclaimed in 1962, and following the initial years of hesitation and conciliatory pronouncements by President Ben Bella who, at the Alexandria Summit in 1964, agreed to make concessions provided that the FLN also gave its agreement, his successor, President Boumediene, adopted an intransigent attitude and only condescendingly agreed to economic cooperation in exchange for recognition of borders as defined by him.

Algeria's intransigence is explainable by the theory of the influence of economic cycles on politics. The soaring oil prices in Algeria, from 1967, allowed the country to massively arm itself with the help of the former Soviet Union, and feel stronger vis à vis its neighbours, even to the point of challenging them directly. The correlation between economic and foreign policy cycles in Algeria has been widely corroborated by other empirical factors. The theory of Joshua Goldstein (1979), one of the most famous specialists in international relations, appears to apply to the Algerian case as indeed economic expansion tends to increase the probabilities of external conflict.

In 1970, Tunisia gave in to Algerian threats: on the one hand, it needed Algerian gas, and on the other hand Algeria practised blackmail by starting to drill for oil at Amat El Borma, Tunisia's only oil field, located between the Tunisian and the Algerian borders, still unclearly delimited at the time. An agreement for joint running of this field and renewed discussions on the gas pipeline designed to supply Tunisia did in fact take place, but the turnabout by the Algerians on the price Tunisia was to pay, initially at the producer rate, made cruelly clear to the Tunisians the true intentions of the Algerian authorities, who were more interested in settling the border problem by a treaty definitively linking Tunisia and excluding it as a potential player in a global regional strategy, rather than ensuring genuine economic cooperation.

The border dispute between Morocco and Algeria was worse and more symptomatic of Algeria's attitude. There is a stark contrast between the high aspirations of His Majesty Mohammed V, his concern to preserve a common future on the one hand, and the Machiavellian policies of the Algerian army general staff and some of the key political decision-makers on the other. The intention was to avoid any obstacle to the Algerian war effort and therefore the very legitimacy of their struggle for independence. As a result, the King of Morocco refused to discuss the border dispute with Paris, although the French authorities had been proposing a settlement, from the time of Morocco's independence and right up until the eve of Algerian independence.

It is said that during a council of ministers chaired by His Majesty Mohammed V, everyone supported the opinion of the King. Only one Moroccan government minister expressed doubts about the commitments made by the Algerian liberation movement.[6] This was indicative of a great deal of realism.

It is true that in 1961, President Farhat Abbas recognized in writing that the borders of Algeria would not be in opposition to those of Morocco. But both the Algerian general staff, and the Algerian National Revolutionary Council, expressed criticism of the agreement signed by President Abbas. The army and defenders of the empire were probably aware that Morocco had a right to claim the vast territory of the Sahara which included Touat, Tidikelt, Gourara and Tindouf, where portraits of the King of Morocco were still in evidence in all businesses and residences. These regions were considered to be Moroccan territory although they had been annexed by French Algeria by unilateral decision of France in 1912, the date of the beginning of the French Protectorate in Morocco. Research by historians of French colonial expansion leaves no doubt about this. The reader can refer to French and American studies, difficult to suspect of favouritism on this issue.

In fact the senior officers as well as certain of the Algerian leadership never had the slightest intention of handing over to Morocco one inch of territory inherited from the colonial era. As soon as the

French army withdrew from a given post, the Algerians occupied it by force even if it had been unanimously recognized as being Moroccan. These attacks by the Algerian army cost Moroccan lives, and led to the "war of the sands" in 1963 when all the so-called socialist states in the Arab world supported Algeria against Morocco. This said a lot about the intentions of the masters of Algeria. One did not have to be a great political strategist to perceive what this meant.

Algiers did everything possible to strengthen its position, deploying all the tricks it could to destabilize Morocco. It became one of the Soviet Union's closest allies in the Third World. It reinforced its links and clan-based solidarity with socialist countries. It embraced Nasserism and all revolutionary movements; it exerted permanent pressure on its borders with Morocco by leading Rabat to believe in an impending Soviet build up in the region. It used blackmail against the King of Morocco by granting asylum and assistance to opponents of the Moroccan regime. The best defence, as they say, is attack.

The meeting in Ifrane in 1969 between His Majesty Hassan II and President Boumediene was held in an attempt to get out of the deadlock in which both countries were entrenched. The meeting at Tlemcen, one year later, led to the creation of a joint commission to settle the border dispute and later move on to the issue of economic cooperation. The Moroccans pushed for kindliness that some people equated to blindness, to the point of handing over some disputed territory. A joint company was created to exploit the Gara Djebilet mine, although its existence was in name only.

1970 was an evident turning point in the expansionist policy of Algeria. From that date, Boumediene understood that nothing was left to be recovered by Algeria and that his country had to find other ways to extend the power and influence of its empire. This led to an irrationally vast economic programme developed on strategic lines. Also in the offing was an aggressive foreign policy the prime objectives of which were regional dominance, at one time ready to ally itself with Libya's Colonel Kadhafi, to whom Boumedienne suggested that the two countries should unite. Boumediene also took advantage of soaring oil prices to continue his imperial policies.

This policy recalls the sadly well-known geopolitical concept of *Lebensraum* or "living space" which was one of the justifications of the Third Reich for expansion in Europe. The expression "economic living space" is not my invention; it belonged to the vocabulary of the leading political strategist Belaïd Abdesslam, Minister under Boumediene and future Prime Minister.

Doing away with or at least reducing the influence of Libya on the Polisario Front to which it provided military and financial support, to use coercive pressure on a great number of states to obtain recognition for a Saharan entity that Algiers would dominate, and place Morocco in a secondary position, was one the components of the Maghrebian policy of Algiers. In fact, ideological justification was nothing less than window dressing for the naïve who believed in the "generosity of the Algerian Revolution", and for the Algerians themselves in order to convince them of the validity of the position of Algiers and the economic deprivation it would have to accept to support the Polisario Front. It should be recalled that the Algerian Army, sure of itself due to its military potential, did not hesitate to participate in the battles of Amgala, between the Polisario Front and the Moroccan armed forces. Only very unsuspecting minds could still continue to believe in the neutrality of Algeria.

The economic program was founded on centralized planning taking inspiration from Stalinism and justified by certain Marxist-leaning French economists consulted by Algiers. This meant nationalization of the key sectors of the economy, notably hydrocarbon production and distribution, banks, the mining sector, the creation of state-owned enterprises, and heavy industrialization as promoted by Belaïd Abdesslam, Minister of Energy, representing the "industrialists division" which supported the Saharan policies of Boumediene. In a famous speech to the American people, President Eisenhower warned against the influence of the military-industrial complex on freedoms and democratic methods.[7] So what can be said about the state-run model of the Boumediene era?

The state-run projects were vastly oversized, not very profitable and did not generate much employment, which explains why Algerians continued to emigrate to France, for lack of jobs. Turnkey factories were purchased overseas; the management and operating costs were irrational. As a matter of fact, these factories rarely exceeded 30% of their output capacity.

In line with this imperial vision, Algeria figured it would be able to produce a sufficient number of industrial goods for the local market but especially to conquer Maghrebian and African markets. Algeria had a right to become a hegemonic power in the region. The result of this irrational and feverish industrialization is well known and finally turned out to be one of the greatest economic disasters of the Africa continent.

Agriculture, which had been the dominant economic sector before independence, was neglected. Farms that had formerly been in the hands of French colons were left to run themselves. The reform was a failure and led to the end of the illusion of complete food self-sufficiency.

It would be a great mistake to think that this economic program was directed toward the well-being of the Algerian people. For the military, the people were never the prime objective of these economic projects or a parameter of the equation that had to be solved. One can wonder if it was ever a concern on their part. The sole issue important to them was silence and submission in exchange for only the very basic means of survival, and they were ready to use violence whenever they deemed it necessary. One cannot fathom a destiny crueler than that of such a proud people being subjected to the scramble for power of its leaders.

Is Algeria an imperial state? Some might ask. Does this idea not contain an element of hyperbole? In my opinion, the answer is yes, without a shadow of doubt. From the outset, let me say that I use the expression not in its usual Marxist interpretation which tends to reduce everything to economic or financial determinism, but rather, the liberal meaning which holds that imperialism, in its widest sense, is basically political and refers to all the expansionist policies of a state and the attempt to subject other people by armed force. The universal principle that underlies the policy of any empire is for peace to reign within the state, and that a potential or actual war be waged outside. The economic explanation of imperialism put forth by Marxists is at best simplistic. Strictly speaking, it is false; all serious research has concluded that, for the colonizing nation, the costs incurred by colonial expansion are greater than the benefits. Only a restricted group appears to benefit. Raymond Aron rightly wrote that economic interests are only a pretext or rationalization and that the deep-rooted cause lies in the drive of a nation for power.[8]

One can apply to Algeria what Hobson, one of the best theorists of imperialism, wrote on this subject. For this analyst and critic of the British Empire, imperialism is "the degradation of authentic nationalism", or "perversion" and "depraved choice of national life".

In my view, there is a structural homology between the nature of power in Algeria and the imperial logic that, although carried by individuals, has a tendency to become autonomous and impose its functional laws. The logic of empire is always to conquer simultaneously and keep a firm hand on territorial successes, consolidate what has been achieved and strengthen the zone of influence. An empire incapable of conquest runs the risk of being conquered itself, dismembered at least due to the centrifugal forces within and the resistance posed by other states to which it constitutes a perpetual threat.

That is a condemned heritage that the objective depositories of the French imperial empire so warmly welcomed and of which they remain the blindfolded prisoners. That is exactly the cross being borne with resignation by the Algerian people.

Quite justifiably, the remark will be made that Empire often brings with it a culture which it tends to unify and spread. Look for instance at China, Greece under Alexander, Rome, the Arab Muslim Empire in times of the Abbasids, etc. The cultural dimension, it is true, is absent from the Algerian case. But the Algerian generals could not care less.[9]

The Habsburg empire is an exception, but generally empires like that of Algeria have essentially autocratic political regimes. Moreover the principle of imperial coherence is derived from force, and the principle of coherence is fear. In Algeria the army, as an arm of power, is used to control the people. Inside the country, Algerian imperialism attaches importance to public ownership which is the sole factor worthy of respect as it claims the major share of revenues which support its designs, and can distribute a part thereof to the population. For the people, there was bread and the circuses, basic consumer goods at low cost, and the great ideological events where the political stars of the revolutionary movement were put on show, like Tito, Fidel Castro, Che Guevara, General Giap, without forgetting the minor bit-part players showing themselves off at Afro-Asian conferences in Algiers.

Has the failure of pseudo-socialist communist ideology and the end of the bipolar system made any difference to Algeria's policies with regard to Morocco and other states in the region? There is no evidence to any change in attitude. Apparently, the term cooperation does not feature in the vocabulary of the Algerian leaders in spite of the promises made so many times in the past, and never brought to fruition. The ideal of cooperation appears to be foreign to the philosophy of the Algerian elite in power. The imperial mind set of the psyche of the leaders condemns them to never really seek cooperation.

Algerian foreign policy provides evidence of an essential constant i.e. that of the drive for power. Formerly, Algeria presented itself as a socialist leader of the Third World and attempted to develop a planned, open and aggressive economy that, it was hoped, would make it possible to initiate conquest of the African continent.

But as socialist discourse is no longer in vogue and industrialization has failed for structural reasons, the leaders of Algeria still dress in the robes of an outdated ideology to conceal as yet unrealized imperial ambitions.

The Algerian military has unabashedly used the international consequences of 9/11/2001 to stifle public opinion and shy away from internal problems it is unable to solve. Probably, it will try to blackmail Europe by using the plentiful gas supplies in the Algerian sub-soil. The old continent will be stuck between Russia to the east and Algeria to the south.

3/ A THEORY OF THE IMPERIAL TEMPTATION: ON STRATOCRACY

This rapid overview of the Algerian position will undoubtedly be unsatisfactory to the political expert or the sociologist in international relations to the extent in which it calls for an explanation that we can only summarize here.

How can we explain the consistency in behaviour of the Algerian leaders in their relations with their immediate neighbours since independence?

How can the subordination of the Algerian economy to the war machine, and the exclusive use of the resources in its sub-soil to boost military power be explained?

Is Algeria not, like the former Soviet Union or Iraq under Saddam Hussein, trying to demonstrate that it can use a large share of excess oil production for maintaining military force instead of improving the living conditions of the population thanks to the steadily growing global resources of the nation?

In international relations, there is a theory that is both crystal clear and remarkably succinct, that the philosophers of the Enlightenment broadly referred to and that the theorists of industrialized society developed. It has it that modern states are in a situation in which only two conditions are possible, either trade or war, but the trend toward one or the other pole of the dichotomy basically depends on the nature of the elite in power. From this perspective, it is not surprising that states run by the military tend to favour bellicose attitudes as opposed to the production of goods and international trade.

Societies led by an industrial elite, bankers, and a "creative" class favour work, innovation, and the generation of wealth. The opposition between a "military spirit" and an "industrial spirit", that so many theorists have evoked since the end of the 18th century, is still pertinent. In his theory of imperialism, Schumpeter, an economist of the Vienna School demonstrated that, contrary to Marxist theory, capitalism by its very essence does not lead to war. Bellicose attitudes are not at all the result of the spirit of capitalism but rather a remnant of the pre-capitalist mentality still deep-rooted in the minds of the governing elite.[10]

Since independence, Algeria has been led by a military "caste". Going further back in history, some historians, probably with reason, say that the military took power in 1956, date of the assassination in Morocco of Abane Ramdane upon orders of the chiefs of the National Liberation Army, the armed branch of the FLN. Abane Ramdane was guilty of only one crime; he promoted the principle of the primacy of politics over the military.

To 1978, date of the death of Colonel Boumediene, the military had officially run the country. The candidacy for president of the republic by Colonel Chadli Bendjedid, his election in 1979 and re-election in 1984 were planned and programmed by "army decision makers " or senior officers. From 1979 to 1988, the clan of General Larbi Belkheir held the reigns of power in Algeria.

After the short interval from 1989 to 1991, during which the Algerian people wrongly believed that the era of democracy had arrived, in late 1990 the army planned to overthrow the government in accordance with a plan devised by the Minister of Defense, General Khaled Nezzar, and carried out in 1992. The High Government Committee, the Algerian term for high political circles, dominated by the military and, the government overseen by Ali Kalfi in June 1992 after the assassination of Boudiaf, was to be led by General Lamine Zeroual in 1994.

Abdelaziz Bouteflika, whom the military called out of retirement in a bid to reassure international opinion and counter the view that it was a suspect regime, was elected President in 1999. His executive assistant—before being named ambassador to Morocco, holding a huge amount of power, was General Belkheir, ex-mentor of the man today considered the strong man of Algeria, Mohamed Mediene, nicknamed Tewfik, Chief of the former military security services, now of

the Department of Investigation and Security. In highly symbolic fash-
ion, the civilian President Bouteflika has recently been elevated to the
highest grade in the army, i.e. Army Corps General. He has no qualms
in combining this post with that of President of the National Liberation
Front (FLN).

Against this there was the attempt by Chadli Bendjedid to loosen
his ties with the army, or even to distance it from political power.
Who could deny the commendable but timid attempts of the Algerian
President? Did he not initiate a reform in early 1984 and try to find a
solution to the problem of the Sahara? Did he not put his country on
the road to economic reform and end up, following the spontaneous
riots of 1988, which shook the country, by setting up a multi-party system, giving Algeria for a time the image of a country moving toward
modern democracy? It would be hypocritical to dismiss the pragma-
tism of Chadli, compared to the fundamentalism of Boumediene.

Chadli tried to professionalize and reorganize the army. He also
partially succeeded in leading his country away from the Warsaw Pact
nations, more for reasons of rationalization of the military apparatus
and its weapons than for any ideological objective. He managed to distance himself from older members of the army who were attached to
socialist orthodoxy, or at least to reduce their influence by promoting
young officers to higher ranks.

However, he failed to de-politicize the army and to restrict it to
its barracks. In spite of its internal divisions that remained subdued
when its interests were in question, it remained at the centre of power
in Algeria. The end of the story is well known: Chadli was overridden
by the army, which took control of the executive even if power was
delegated to a civilian government in a bid to save appearances.

It would be a mistake to believe that the army would only have
come back to power after relinquishing it to civilians, in order to
deal with the chaos that would have followed a victory of the Islamic
Salvation Front in the municipal elections of 1990 and the first round
of legislative elections in 1991, and opt for a *pronunciamiento*. This picture, as reassuring as it may be, does not correspond to the historical
or political truth. In fact the Algerian army entered the political sphere
at the end of the 1950s and since then has never left. "Can we trust
the people?"—asked a French revolutionary after 9 Thermidor (27 July
1794). The permanent state of emergency in Algeria which violates the
principles of all democratic constitutions, constitutes a clear response
to that question. Experts in military sociology have not considered the

special status of the Algerian army, which once and for all has over-
taken entire sovereignty in the name of the people.

The army is certainly not that "guardian of the City", which is
supposed to be under the orders of the philosopher kings, in other
words those who know the ultimate ends. It is not even the institution which diverges most from political power and society, according to the pessimistic vision of Samuel Huntington. It is more than a
pressure or even veto group. It is the state. The ministerial council is
nothing more than an executive body in charge of the administration
and application of the major orientations defined by the army. The
judiciary has no freedom and little social status, apart from its moral
standing, and is permitted merely to look after minor disputes among
the common people instead of application of the law as is the rule in
any legitimate state.

The sociology of the elite and of social networks constitute precious tools for grasping the reality of the Algerian military hierarchy:
the senior officers of the army recruit each other, thereby constituting
a caste whose roots are to be found in the triangle formed by Batna,
Tebessa, and Souk-Ahrass. At the highest levels, it constitutes a dense,
homogenous and highly complex network. The nomination of officers
to the heads of military regions or any other sensitive area is accom-
plished according to the principle of loyalty and co-optation. Any diver-
gence in opinion that may arise between senior officers is resolved in
conclaves. Any decision taken at these meetings implicates the commitment of all. No one knows the criteria according to which anyone
participates in such meetings. From a sociological standpoint, this is
readily understandable, for after all the senior officers of European
armies were also typically formed historically from a caste of individuals originating in the aristocratic classes. That is true, but as opposed
to the Algerians, they were not hostile to democratic ideas and did not
question the principle of the legitimacy of political modernity. What
Algerian General MacArthur would accept being removed from office
by the civilian authorities?

Who runs Algeria? Asks the political sociologist. In Algeria, the
power elite consists of a homogeneous group dominating the entire
social system thanks to the control it wields over military, economic
and political institutions. The triangle of power is constituted by the
Army, the FLN and the leaders of the major state-run enterprises chosen according to the criteria laid down by the military. At the top
of this institutional triangle sits the army which controls the other

institutions. This is really a "stratocracy", a neologism coined from the Greek "*stratos*", the army, and *kratos*, or power, to take account of the special character of the regime.[11]

As opposed to democracies or even to countries in democratic transition where the political game of the pluralistic elite consists of striking a balance between diverging interests, in Algeria power is concentrated in the hands of a caste.[12] The power structure in Algeria has the form of a stratified pyramid, not in three or four stages, but rather in two: with the senior army officers and a few FLN leaders at the top who enjoy all power and the base consisting of a mass society that has no other way of expressing itself than through revolt and protest. There are no multiple decision-making centres as in democratic societies, and no veto group can emerge. Only one unified, homogeneous centre of power with common interests was built up during the national liberation war, and this still continues. It can define the political problems and solutions that should be adopted, whether for domestic or foreign policy. Any opposition between individuals belonging to this circle is rare and remains secret, without effect on political life. The solidarity reigning within is essentially that of the clan.[13] Hence, one should not be surprised that immorality and corruption proliferate.

In Algeria, the senior military officers have confiscated freedom, imposed a single party system, the reign of the sword rather than of the law, terror and violence rather than dialogue. Over the past few years, they have accepted the existence of political organizations provided they do not question their power. The most elementary human rights are ignored, and often violated. Intellectuals, journalists, magistrates are assassinated or condemned to exile. Whether directly or not, the senior officers contributed greatly to the aggravation of the civil war which cost nearly 150 000 deaths in Algeria. It may be salutary to recall that the Algerian army and other services had their own version of the armed Islamic groups.

In Algeria, things occur like in other nations. So long as the military caste dominates both state and society, work will not be socially or economically valued: production and productive forces will be subordinate to military power. It has been common knowledge for a long while that the views of Algerian Military Security have been decisive in determining the appointment of personnel to top administrative posts, of diplomats, of the leaders of large public enterprises, and even of members of the government. This is illustrated by two factors, one

macrosociological and the other macroeconomic, as well as the tute-
lary power of the Algerian army and its effects.

Firstly, no one would be surprised to learn that the Algerian Army
continues to massively attract the most brilliant secondary-school
graduates. In spite of the degradation in the image of the military
institutions, and in spite of the high risks run by the Algerian military
since the beginning of the civil war, the young Algerian usually opts
for top military schools because he knows that a university degree will
be of no use on the job market, while the army provides a good salary,
benefits in kind, promotion, or even an opportunity to get rich if he
accepts the laws of the Mafia.

The gendarmerie and police also attract the young. By the end of
this decade, the police will have 200,000 members versus 45,000 in the
early 1980s. A constant change in the social structure of the military
establishment has been evident. Officers fresh out of the top schools
are, in their majority, from the middle classes, as opposed to their elders
who come from the lower middle classes. This concerns private soldiers
as much as the officer class. All units combined, it is estimated the
security forces number about 550,000 members. Rational choice theory
readily explains these results as shown by recent studies on Algeria.

Secondly, in spite of the notable reforms that the Algerian economy
has undergone over the past few years, the success of the structural
adjustment policy, the drastic reduction in the budgetary deficit, the
sharp drop in the external debt, the massive investment and plan for
supporting growth over five years amounting to 55 billion dollars, the
Algerian economy basically remains dependent on investment income,
distribution-oriented and unproductive.

Creative and job-generating investments are not enough to make
up for endemic unemployment which affect 30% of the active population (60% for the young), or to offer employment each year to the
300,000 new arrivals on the job market. The Algerian economy is experiencing countless difficulties. Infrastructures have reached a surrealistic
state of decay, water management remains unknown; agriculture, probably because it requires too much effort, has been neglected in spite
of a few notable experiments. The rise in per capita income of more
than 31% in two years, according to the National Statistics Office, is
non detectable when observing the conditions of daily life of the citizen, housing is in extremely limited supply, and the most basic social
services are incapable of meeting citizens' demand. Only schooling and
education in the countryside constitute an important advance.

On the other hand, Algeria offers a great counter-example of the *ethos* of work in a modern economy. The problem of the Algerian economy is not of a financial order as the country benefits from huge profits from oil and gas. It is, rather, about the value attached to work. The ethics of work and production, in my view, is indicative of three major problem areas of the economy of the country, i.e. the emergence of the private sector whose share in production is too modest, the pervasiveness of hydrocarbons, as well as corruption, principally due to the client-oriented approach of the army, penalizes private economic actors as well as consumers. In 2006, Algeria's growth rate was probably no more than 3%, even though officially it was declared to be 6%.[14]

Is it possible to get rid of clientilism, the private preserve of an economy governed by the principle of Mafiosi gain and to which all sectors are subject?

Max Weber, the master of German sociology, demonstrated that so long as an economy has not become a sphere of autonomous activity, so long as it is not a coherent system, a *cosmos* endowed with its own logic and impervious to the influence of other spheres of activity such as politics, religion or the military, it will not be able to reach the degree of rationality so characteristic of capitalism.

Tired of waiting for deliverance, tired of bearing the heavy burden of the army for more than four decades, many Algerians hope for a "velvet revolution", the advent of a providential person who could offer stability and the democratization of society. The Algerian people should recall what Lenin said: "no revolution is possible against the army".

But of what importance to the generals are the people who suffer from their actions? Literature, especially German, gives edifying insight. At the beginning of a scene in *Mother Courage and her children*, the sergeant expresses the militarist point of view that the German political left attributed to Prussian officers in the time of the Kaiser. Bertold Brecht has him say: *"Frieden, das ist nur Schlamperei, erst der Krieg schafft Ordnung"* ["peace is nothing other than pandemonium, only war gives rise to order"]. Brecht, who was traumatized by World War I when he was only twenty, devoted his best songs to armed conflicts but also expressed the views of German intellectuals during the first years of the Weimar Republic, that the military caste always exploits the lower social classes.

It would be less of a risk for the Algerians to rely on their resources and the promise of a truly open economy. It would transfer its own rationality to other spheres of activity; it would gradually make Algeria enter a modernity beneficial to both Algerians and their neighbours. Cooperation and economic trade will get the edge over factors determining the level of hostility. Let us hope that the emergence of the Nedroma, Tlemcen, and Maghnia triangle, from which the new economic actors originate, will counterbalance, if only partially, the militarist triangle.

The contemporary history of the West demonstrates that work is the sole producer of wealth and peace. This is the point at which to draw the obvious lessons from this precedent, and hope to enter a era of economic rationality and reason-based action.

In his famous philosophical essay entitled *Project for perpetual peace*, written in 1794, at the end of the Enlightenment, Emmanuel Kant states, in accordance with liberals such as Adam Smith, that democratic states are destined to participate less often in armed conflicts than autocratic states. He bases his theory on the principle of instrumental rationality. Because, he argues, it is the citizens who have to support the cost of war by paying taxes and sacrificing their lives. In a democracy where they largely control the decisions that are made, war tends to be avoided. On the other hand, in autocratic states, the decision makers are more likely to opt for war, because they do not have to suffer the cost of it. In this way, they maximize their utility. Contemporary research tends to support this theory, even though it demonstrates that the relationship between the nature of power and wars is less strong than the theory would predict. This shows, however, that armed conflicts are much less frequent between democracies. Peace results from both instrumental rationality and the axiological rationality that expresses common values.

4/ STRATEGIC CONSEQUENCES: *PAX ALGERIANA*

It is said of Algeria that it constitutes itself by opposition. It is constantly looking for a positional enemy, according to the expression in *Peace and War between nations*, where Raymond Aron applied it to the United States and the former Soviet Union. Algeria believes it is forging its unity by the representation of a world and system of values inevitably opposing it to other societies. We should beware that ideologies lead us to what August Comte called 'wars of principles', which are the worst of all.

We can understand that the Algerian authorities hold very dear the principle of self-determination and the right of a people to independence which they would like to see applied to the Sahara even if the International Court of Justice issued a clear-cut statement on the links uniting this province to Morocco, and the treaties dating from before Spanish colonization, leaving no doubt as to the sovereignty of the King of Morocco over the Sahara, and secondarily the material and procedural impossibility of such a referendum.

To those who deem the principle of self-determination to be intangible and require that it be systematically applied everywhere, it would be salutary to recall that in Evian in 1962, Algeria indignantly rejected a French proposal favouring consultation with the Touaregs.

But doesn't this argument mask geostrategic and economic ambitions? With access to the sea on the Mediterranean only, it can be appreciated that Algeria wants to reduce the cost of its gas and oil exports by enjoying an outlet on the Atlantic. It is also supposed that it wanted to dispose of a vassal state in the Sahara rather than a full-fledged economic partner—by definition less inclined to docility. But who would accept such a solution catering to the point of view of just one state to the detriment of all the others?

This is not a game. The birth of a state completely under the control of Algeria would wind up destroying the political balance in the region. Algeria would be in control of the entire Saharan arch and would become the predominant power in the region. This solution would satisfy what I have described as the imperial *Hubris*. Moreover, the Greater Middle East would be dominated to the West by a power whose future is unpredictable, especially when considering its recent or even more distant past. Mauritania could be threatened in the long run, and reduced to becoming nothing more than the satellite of a new great power. Its natural reserves, especially of oil, would be subjected to indirect political control. Neither Tunisia, Libya nor the countries neighbouring the Sahara (Mali, Niger, Chad) in the long run would know any other peace than the *pax algeriana*.

Morocco is a key country in this equilibrium. If it were weakened, if a part of the Sahara were cut off from it, if it were reduced to becoming a state subjected to a constant threat on its southern borders, it would lose its entire strategic capacity to contribute to peace and equilibrium of the Greater Middle East.

Who would dare predict today the future of the configuration of the states of the Greater Middle East? Who would be in a position to measure or to predict the internal evolution on the international chessboard? In the area of international relations, it is normal to always envisage the worst, although what is happening before our eyes could be considerably less grave that what might occur in the future.

To the east of the Greater Middle East, the power of Iran, newly acquired, is already overtaking Iraq, Syria, and Lebanon, and probably the future Palestine. We have witnesses to its capacity for causing unrest in Lebanon and Iraq. Its ambitions can be correctly interpreted only when taking into consideration its determination to become a regional power. It is likely to become a direct threat to several countries in the Near East or, at the very least, it could attempt to extend its influence over them if a coalition including Pakistan to the east and Morocco to the west were not true pillars counterbalancing its force. It would not stop while following such an encouraging path. Saudi Arabia, the Gulf States, and Jordan will soon become a part of its zone of influence and would be threatened by internal unrest due to clever manipulation of the numerous Shiite minorities residing there. The leaders of these countries have fully understood this for some time and believe that they have to respond to the Iranian threat by creating a coalition with Egypt, so long as it does not fall into the hands of governments under fundamentalist control.

Neither Libya, Tunisia nor Algeria constitutes fixed and reasonably sure points. Leading indicators suggest that the regimes of Colonel Kaddafi in Libya and President Ben Ali in Tunisia are facing immense problems and endemic protest. This may turn out to be a continual and strong fundamentalist threat that years of repression have not managed to contain, the said trends reconstituting like the ashes of a phoenix. We know about the force of such movements in Tunisia and the exorbitant political cost they bring. Even Libya is a part of this trend. Consideration should be given to recent reports about the unfortunate foreign doctors and nurses, wrongly suspected of having inoculated Aids into Libyans although the results of research showed they could never have been guilty of doing anything of the sort. The Libyan authorities fear the reaction of the Islamists, whatever it decides to do: it is fearful of the criticism of its health policies, which neglect the hospitals, even though it is resigned to the truth, and is alarmed by the accusations of weakness that will be inevitably lodged against it if it increases the number of these unfortunate people that the vicissitudes of life have led to an inhospitable land.

In today's Algeria the moderate Islamists have accepted a slice of power that the military have granted, via a fragile agreement, while it remains thwarted by fundamentalist movements who are far from having been disarmed and who have managed to burrow deep within Algerian society. The appointment at the helm of the Algerian government of Abdelaziz Belkhadem—an apparatchik of the FLN of which he is the general secretary (single party of independence from 1962 to 1989), head of an Islamic tendency within the FLN, influenced by certain aspects of the ideology of the Muslim Brotherhood, favourable to the integration of former insurgents of the Islamic Salvation Front, could never have occurred without the blessing of the military.

What will be the outcome of the hidden struggle between the various forces in power in Algeria? What is the future of the centrifugal forces that could smash the unity of this country? The Kabyle rebellion may be a forerunner to significant change. The burgeoning claims of the Kabyle people—who compare themselves to the Kurds of Iraq—are beginning to be heard.

Mauritania is also in the throes of a struggle for power between the modernist tendency and the fundamentalist forces. The premiss of democratization could be overturned at any moment by the forces of obscurantism.

In this unstable configuration, Morocco appears as a moderate state, politically stable especially since the late 1980s when the socialists rid themselves of their antiquated ideas and converted to political and economic liberalism. Even the Party of Justice and Development, homonym of the party currently ruling Turkey, share the fundamental values around which a national consensus has emerged.

Morocco has always been a sure and special ally of the Arab Gulf States across the Arab peninsula. Its military cooperation with these countries goes back decades. Its commitments toward its allies have always been respected. Its position within NATO makes it a trustworthy ally capable of assuming its responsibilities in case of crisis.

The scope and stakes involved in the event of war between Morocco and Algeria, will be of concern to all of the world's powers. What would happen in the event of armed conflict? The consequences would be disastrous: both countries would be ruined, weakened and perhaps destroyed, dismembered, and extremist groups would profit from this situation to muster their forces to create instability across the board. This hegemonic war, by becoming a "war of principles" according to the apt expression of Auguste Comte, would release ultra-nationalist forces, influenced by fundamentalist ideologies and cast real demons into the city. The victory of one of the two belligerents would inevitably lead to their hegemony over the entire region. The great powers are aware of this.

In fact, only the military caste would benefit from the tensions it creates and continuously fans. The only thing that counts for it is power, total domination domestically and a virtual war externally, without any true cause or ethic of responsibility. The historian and sociologist would be entirely ready to understand this imperial temptation if it was at least the source of an authentic culture on the verge of expansion. The Chinese, Indian, Greek, Roman, Byzantine, and Arabo-Muslim empires all had a cultural dimension. But the arrogant gestures and vain claims of the policy of power are the ideas of superficial and mediocre minds, definitively recalcitrant to any cultural significance in human activity.

Ares, the god of war in the Greek pantheon, paid no attention to the justice of the cause he supported. Actually he does not have any. His violence, anger, his acts of cruelty could certainly be fought by reason. But will Athena come down once against from Olympus to contain them?

NOTES

In this chapter, I contrast two typical and ideal cultures of power that, from my perspective, seem recalcitrant even though the civil societies from which they spring share several cultural, historical and religious backgrounds. The first stresses democracy, human rights, economic liberalism, and to a certain degree the work *ethos* for the production of material and intellectual goods. The second, on the other hand, is characterized by a secret policy controlled by senior officials of the army, the use of huge natural resources of their country's subsoil for arming, corrupting, and subjecting citizens, and the exercise of a permanent mistrust in their regard.

1. The passage by Montesquieu is excerpted from chapter XVII of book 19 of *The Spirit of laws* (Eng. trs. Thomas Nugent, 1752), entitled "The augmentation of troops". Indeed, Montesquieu not only perfectly understood the mechanisms of the arms race but he also showed that one of its consequences is strategic alliances. The remainder of the text is very clear on this point: "Great princes, not satisfied with hiring or buying troops of petty states, make it their business on all sides to pay subsidies for alliances, that is, generally to throw away their money."
2. In *The Peloponnesian War*, Thucydides distinguishes between grievances and disputes, the deep-rooted war by the opposite party. In book I, XXIII, 6 he writes "The truest cause is also the least admitted: in my opinion the Athenians, by growing in numbers, give rise to concern to the Lacedemonians, forcing them into war". On this subject, see the remarkable *Thucydide et l'impérialisme athénien* by Jacqueline de Romilly.
3. A convenient but formalized presentation of the arms race is found in a book by Anatol Rapoport (1960). Based on a simple theoretical model of two differential

equations taking into consideration the rate of growth in arms expenditures of two countries, the grievances and restrictive factors constituted by the excessive costs resulting from greater expenditures for armaments, Rapoport deduces propositions about the conditions of stable and unstable equilibrium of the system of relations between the two countries, the arms race, and mutual disarmament, etc. He applies his model to a real case, that of Europe on the eve of the First World War, and proves the pertinence thereof by comparing the predictions allowed by the model and the data of Richardson.

I will summarize briefly here the fundamental properties of the structure of the prisoner's dilemma and the game of "chicken". I will also refer to some historical data and policies concerning relations between Morocco and Algeria that can be hypothetically subsumed within one or other game.

The expression "Prisoner's dilemma" is attributed to A.W. Tucker, who conceived the following example to illustrate the structure of the game. Two prisoners are suspected of having committed a crime. The judge suggests the following: 5 years of jail if they both confess to their crime, a lighter sentence if they do not confess to the crime, or acquittal for the one who does confess to the crime, if the other does not, and 10 years for the one who does not confess.

Let us suppose that two people, I and J, each have the choice of two strategies: A to cooperate or B to not cooperate. The general structure of the prisoner's dilemma can be translated by the following matrix. The numbers are, of course, invented. They correspond to the possible gains of both players. The first number of each pair represents the gain (positive number) or loss (negative number) of the first player, the second number refers to those of the second player.

		J	
		A	B
I	A	5, 5	−10, 10
	B	10, −10	−5, −5

The combination of the two strategies gives rise to four possible results, AA, AB, BA and BB. The order of preference of individual I is: BA > AA, AA > BB and BB> AB. It is more beneficial for him not to cooperate if J does (BA > AA) than to cooperate. In this case, I will have a gain equal to 10 and J an equivalent loss. If I does not cooperate, his gain (10) will be greater than that he would have achieved if he had cooperated (5). But he prefers to cooperate if J cooperates instead of the situation where both players do not cooperate (AA > BB). By cooperating, I and J will come out with a gain equal to 5, while if they fail to cooperate, all will register a loss equal to 5. I will opt not to cooperate if J does not, rather than cooperating alone (BB > AB). I prefers a loss of 5 for himself and for J rather than to lose 10 where J gains just as much.

The order of preference of J is: AB > AA, AA > BB and BB > BA. Both players agree only on the two intermediate situations placing AA and BB in position 2 and 3, but they are in total disagreement for the first and the fourth. The dominant strategy is therefore non-cooperation, even if for both parties it is more costly than cooperation.

This game has two distinctive characteristics:

1/ Strategy B is dominant for both players: for each possible choice of one of the players, it provides the other with a gain above that procured by A.
2/ The resulting choice of these dominant strategies, (BB), is less than optimal as it involves fewer gains for the two players than result (AA).

These two characteristics are the source of the "dilemma": the fact that A and B each have a dominant strategy leads to each opting for it, especially seeing that each one knows that the other has a dominant strategy and knows that the other also knows that he has one, etc. But the choice, which is to an extent inevitable, of a dominant strategy by both players, leads to a less than optimal outcome (the "prisoners" condemn each other while it would be in their interest not to confess to the crime). Here the "dilemma" is due to the fact that the model has only one Nash equilibrium which is less than optimal.

The tragedy of the game is that each of the two players cannot allow cooperation because each risks considerable losses if one cooperates and the other does not. Any measure of cooperation would be exploited by the adversary. Cooperation does not necessarily emerge spontaneously even when the game is repeated and if each player deems that the other cannot tolerate cooperation in the future, assuming that both are rational and capable of calculating the effect of the choice of one will have over the choice of the other.

The game of "chicken" is inspired by the situation where two young people challenge each other to a mutual test. On a main road, each gets behind the steering wheel of a car parked at some distance from the other, before heading toward each other. Both cars are bound to cause a head-on impact if one of the two players (or both simultaneously) fails to swerve away from the other car to avoid crashing. The one who swerves will be deemed to be "chicken". Non-cooperation is fatal to both players.

The structure of the "chicken" game is represented by the following matrix. The numbers representing gains and losses were changed to clarify the game.

		J	
		A	B
I	A	0, 0	−10, 10
	B	10, −10	−20, −20

Note that there is a substantial difference between the two matrices.

As in the case of the prisoner's dilemma, the combination of the two strategies gives rise to four possible results AA, AB, BA and BB. The order of preference of individual I is: BA > AA, AA > AB and AB > BB. The order of preference of J is: AB > AA, AA > BA and BA > BB. It is more beneficial for I not to cooperate if J cooperates, than in the situation where both players cooperate (BA > AA): in the first configuration, I wins 10 and J loses 10; in the second, there is no loss but no gain either. I prefers the situation where both players cooperate than the one where he cooperates and J does not. I will opt to cooperate even if J does not, rather than create a situation where both fail to cooperate (AB > BB). The dominant strategy is therefore cooperation.

In the "chicken" game, there are two equilibriums (AB) and (BA). The theory makes it impossible to predict the behaviour of the players. Everything depends on the representation that player A has of player B and vice-versa. If one of the two players deems that the other is "chicken", he will choose strategy B with the ensuing head-on impact.

All indications are that since the independence of Algeria in 1962 and the accession of Hassan II to the throne in 1962, Morocco and Algeria have both felt they were in a form of the "chicken" game. Both defended what they considered to be their territorial integrity. Algeria began by conceding economic advantages and committed itself to help Morocco recover the Western Sahara at the same time pushing Morocco to gradually recognize the *status quo* of the borders inherited from French colonization.

Once Algeria was in a position to impose its point of view on Morocco, it hardened its position and became intransigent. To add insult to injury, it entered into an alliance with the Moroccan left and helped either directly or indirectly in the plot of 1963 against King Hassan II. The "war of the sands" of 1963 was a consequence of the "chicken" game where each side suffers unnecessary losses. In any case this was Ben Bella's view, as a year later, he sent an emissary to Rabat to suggest economic concessions to the king in respect of the territorial claims lodged by Morocco. Better yet, in an interview with the king of Morocco, the Algerian President accepted reconsideration of the border dispute in 1965 and proposed still more economic concessions.

The situation changed with the Algerian coup d'état and grab for power by Colonel Boumediene. Then the conflict took on the form of the prisoner's dilemma. Algeria armed massively with the help of the former Soviet Union, nationalized the mines which had been agreed to be under joint exploitation by both countries, as they were on a border still unclearly drawn, and openly aided the Moroccan opposition. The requests by Morocco and Tunisia for UN arms control in the Maghreb remained a dead letter. This led to an arms race easier for Algeria to afford because of its oil, than by Morocco which followed but whose military expenditures harmed its finances and had a direct effect on its economic and social projects.

But in 1969, Morocco abandoned its territorial claims by getting Boumediene to accept its help in recovering the Western Sahara from Spanish rule. As of that date, Algeria considered Morocco to be a weak state incapable of defending itself militarily. It thought the regime in Morocco was all the more uncertain because of the coup attempts in July 1971 and August 1972 against the king of Morocco (which according to some sources, Algeria supported) and which were expected to succeed and thus bring the military leaders to power. So here, we returned to a form of the "chicken" game in which Morocco was doomed to cooperate without any assurance of cooperation on the part of its adversary. As it happens, Algeria systematically played the strategy of non-cooperation, in particular, by arming itself and, from the time of its independence deliberately assisting all opponents to the Moroccan monarchy, be they different factions or the Polisario Front.

So, for more than a decade, Hassan II gave the impression to the Algerian authorities that Morocco had good intentions and a policy of reconciliation by proposing settlement of border disputes by negotiation and accepting substantial territorial concessions that only reinforced the beliefs of the Algerian military. The Algerian military authorities interpreted the diplomatic endeavours of the king of Morocco as proof of the weakness of the Moroccan regime which, let us recall, was subject to constant hostility by left wingers who never believed in the virtues of democracy, and by certain senior officers, who spent most of their time preparing plans to overthrow the regime overthrows and ultimately carrying them out, although with no positive results for themselves.

In the view of the Algerian general staff, by systematically playing for a time the strategy of cooperation and reconciliation, Morocco gave the impression that it was involved in the "chicken" game structure and preferred to suffer the effects of aggression to avoid the catastrophe that would have been provoked by a war. Relations between Morocco and Algeria precisely illustrate the combination of two game structures. As of 1975, the two protagonists were in the prisoner's dilemma game structure.

In my view the history of the complex relations between Algeria and Morocco, barely outlined here, is a good counter example of one of the propositions of some game theorists for whom a repeated game leads to cooperation, as it is the only rational solution. At any rate, this is what Rapoport (1965), Axelrod (1984) argue. The proposition may be true, but it is definitely not so unconditionally. An iterative game does not necessarily lead to cooperation because the risks induced by failure to cooperate by the adversary are not so great that the political decision-makers of both countries are doomed to play it indefinitely. This was the situation for the two main superpowers up to the collapse of the Soviet Empire. To find a solution, an external element was necessary to break the chains of the vicious circle in which the adversaries were enmeshed. It is possible to argue that but for this solution, victory would have gone to the adversary the most prepared to stick it out for the longest time. But here, we enter into the universe of the legitimacy of sacrifice and ideology. In other words, we leave the realm of instrumental rationality for that of axiological rationality.

4. The "Strategic Defense Initiative", launched in 1983 by President Reagan and his security advisors, consisted of giving the United States an anti-missile space shield capable of neutralizing any enemy missile before it reached American territory. If it had materialized, the programme would have transformed the

United States into a non-attackable sanctuary. It was so costly that the Soviets were powerless to continue confronting the escalating military expenditures. They abandoned the game. The essence of this programme was to question the doctrine of the balance of terror which dominated relations between east and west since 1949, and therefore to exit the structure of the prisoner's dilemma. It is not without reason that this programme was christened "Star Wars"; because it was, indeed, sheer utopia. But the Soviets could neither know this or doubt the determination of the United States. On this subject, see Boudon (2003). Officially the United States dropped the project in 1993 and replaced it with another more modest one focusing on anti-missile defense. Recent events, in particular the strides made by Chinese technology and the now undeniable arms race in space, led them to reconsider American vulnerability and to push further ahead on the very costly anti-missile programme. This is one of the reasons for their determination to install a missile shield in Europe.

5. In Greek thought, ὕβρις or *hybris* is the personification of disproportion, the feeling of unlimited confidence in one's own force which infringes on the law that the gods of the Pantheon devised for humans. Therefore, it is blasphemous and calls for divine vengeance. Everything that rises above this condition and threatens social order and the equilibrium of the cosmos is condemned to punishment meted out by Nemesis, the daughter of the night. The Greeks, notably Hesiod in *Works and Days*, sees it as in opposition to justice. Hesiod shows that based on the myth of the cycle of races, that the disproportion practised by the silver and bronze races, leads inevitably to misfortune, and justice, which is the essence of the gold races and heroes, consolidates social order. Contrary to what some might believe, this notion and its ethical correlates are not the inventions of Greek thought. They can be found in ancient Mesopotamian thought also, particularly with regard to one of the very first instances of writing of all humanity in the Akkadian age of the third millennium before our era, which recounts the adventures of an ancient king of Ourouk, Gilgamesh, and also the dramatic history of all humanity. Further to the unceasing prayers of humans, tired of the ravages caused by king Gilgamesh and Enkidu, a character from the primitive ages of humanity, friend of the King and companion of heroic combats, and also further to the disproportion of the two heroes unable to stop themselves on time to avoid offending the gods, together they joined to condemn one of themselves to death. For more on the subject of disproportion in the sage of Gilgamesh, see Labat (1970).

6. I owe this information to a minister of His Majesty who was kind enough to enlighten me on these issues. I can never fully express my own debt to him in this respect, and what everyone who knows him owes to this exceptional personality.

7. On the military/industrial complex, reference should be made to the classic study of C. Wright Mills (1956)

8. On imperialism and the explanation thereof by Marxists, many references exist. See in particular Cain (2002), Brewer (1984), Owen and Sutcliffe (1981 eds). The theory presented here will be seen to differ from that of Hardt and Negri (2000) and Mann (2003) to the extent that I consider their thesis of end of nation-state

sovereignty and the emergence of a global imperial power is a reality in appearance alone. They do not devote sufficient attention to the creation of great regional powers.

9. On this point, is it interesting to read the reflections of Mommsen (1981) and Baechler (2006).

10. In fact, I allude here to a series of theories and hypotheses on the relationships between the economic, the political and the military. Firstly, the theory developed by *The Spirit of Laws*. Montesquieu says that trade, in particular international trade, goes hand in hand with a reduction in tensions and violence. He writes in chapter II of Book XX: "Peace is the natural effect of trade. Two nations who traffic with each other become reciprocally dependent; for if one has an interest in buying, the other has an interest in selling: and thus their union is founded on their mutual necessities." Similar ideas are found among the Scottish philosophers, in particular Adam Smith, Adam Ferguson and John Millar, as well as James Stuart. The essay by Hirschman (1977) is essential reading on this subject.

I also refer to the theories of Saint Simon and August Comte on the evolution of modern day societies, which were taken up by Herbert Spencer, Durkheim and partially by Schumpeter. The theorists of industrial society emphasised above all the incompatibility between the military spirit and the spirit that underlies industrial society. It can be argued that this theory is too dogmatic, as is shown by Raymond Aron in *Industrial Society and War*. Many other assumptions by Comte, in particular on national wars, without doubt the most ruinous and implacable due to their emotional and ideological foundations, turned out to be untrue. However, it cannot be denied that industrial society enables more cooperation and makes war if not impossible at least unreasonable, even if it makes the relationship between the economic and the military more dialectic .

A fundamental point to be underscored here is the relative specificity of the relationship between empire and war, which sheds a singular light on the Algerian case.

11. The term "stratocracy" applicable to any political regime of a military nature consisting of two Greek words, στρατιά, army and κρατος power.

12. The role of the military in non-democratic regimes has been the subject of a considerable sociological literature, especially by Janowitz (1962), Huntington (1968), and Rouquié (1982) on Latin America. For the period of democratic transition, see O'Donnell, Schmitter and Whitehead (1986).

13. The homogeneity of the Algerian general staff is radically different from the heterogeneity of the American Army as a pressure group described by Janowitz (1960) along the same lines as the analyses of Huntington, to give only one example.

14. References to Algerian foreign policy are many indeed. I will refer to a handful here: Husson (1960), Martel (1965), Amsden (1968), Trout (1969), Ammour (1971), Leca and Katin (1974), Etienne (1977), Balta and Rulleau (1978), Dessens (1978), Yafseh (1982), Damis (1983), Grimaud (1984), Villiers (1987), Gallisot (1988), Brahimi (1990), Blin (1990), Addi (1990), Lamchichi (1991), Leveau (1993), Stora (1995). Nor are to be forgotten the testimonies and studies by Maazouzi (1976, 1977, 1978, 2004), Mohsen-Fenan (1997, 2002 ed.).

2

The State in Crisis

On Tribal Temptation and the De-territorialization of Terrorism

This short chapter poses some questions about the relationship between failures of the State, the de-territorialization of terrorism, the tribal temptations of political movements and certain consequences for internal and external security in different countries. It does not pretend to be original, as that would indeed require perfect knowledge of the subjects dealt with, as well as sociological imagination fed by lengthy meditation.

I do not set out to propose solutions to regional or global problems that others, better qualified than me, might suggest. The few milestones planted in this chapter are, at the most, reference points preparing the way to future reflection.

Many signs lead one to believe that the state is everywhere experiencing, perhaps not an eclipse, but polymorphous protest: it is no longer able to assume its functions and traditional roles, in the economic, political or security spheres. Globalization, the de-territorialization of terrorism, and repeated failures by the state to satisfy social needs, are all indices leading some circles to predict the end of the state as we know it today. Faced with the threat of international terrorism, worried about their own security and that of others, the great powers have realised that no country can ever be an impermeable sanctuary, and have taken the initiative to apply the principle of interference so as to act with the agreement of the States concerned.

One also is aware of the concomitant awakening of nationalism, regionalism and tribalism challenging the state in several ways. This is a phenomenon to which some sociologists have called attention. I will refer only to one. In a remarkable, short but significant article published on the eve of his death, Ernest Gellner (1998) called attention to the historical specificity of this problem by proposing a few areas of research. He also tried to develop assumptions about the remarkable resistance and force of Islam that, for him, was the great enigma of the end of the last century, and the start of new.

Let there be no mistake: I make no amalgamation nor do we draw any "obvious" link between these emerging concerns. Who could forget the lesson of the Scottish philosopher, David Hume, who always reminded us of the fact that the concomitance of events does not signify causality? All these problems are posed simultaneously and call for careful consideration.

Elsewhere I have suggested an outline for an interpretation of Islamic fundamentalism. The other questions I pose focus more on tensions engendered by the failures of the state, the centrifugal movements threatening them and their consequences. I shall limit myself to the Maghreb.

1/ CRISIS OF THE STATE, AMERICAN AND FRENCH INITIATIVES

Until the late 1990s, the Western doctrine predominating in international relations was that the Maghreb is principally in the European sphere of influence and that it should play a key role within it. This theory which made it possible to interpret the facts and to direct action, no longer corresponds to new international realities. Indeed, since 1998, upon the initiative of Eizenstat, the undersecretary of state for the economy and foreign affairs in the Clinton Administration, the Maghreb was no longer considered as a peripheral zone. According to the Eizenstat report, due to its strategic geographical position, its population and markets, its economic potential and greater openness of the institutions of these countries, the Maghreb has become a central partner of the American economy.

Moreover, since 9/11 2001 and the terrorist attacks on targets situated on American soil, economic cooperation between the United States and the Maghreb has gone hand in hand with a strengthening of links in the field of security. The terrorist incidents in Casablanca, Spain and London, and the fears of mounting radical Islamic fundamentalism throughout the region threatening American, European and North African interests, led to the tightening of the ties between the American Department of Defense and the armed forces of the Maghreb. Among the obvious signs of the growing interest of the United States in this region, one can recall the increase in American aid to the Maghreb, the official visit of American civilian and military officials to the countries of the region, the increase in the number of military manoeuvres and, in particular, the significant presence of Moroccan units in NATO manoeuvres in the Mediterranean. In 2004, the United States granted Morocco the status of preferential non-member ally in NATO, thereby allowing this country to participate in American research and development programs in the field of defense.

But it is especially since the United States realized that the Sahel has become a zone of insecurity, weapons trafficking, drugs and high population, i.e. a base for terrorist groups linked to Al Qaida, that they were concerned to promote initiatives whose purpose is to eradicate this evil. Drawing lessons from Afghanistan's role as a safe haven for terrorist groups, the United States has attempted to make this zone secure, and more generally the greater Middle East itself, from the Atlantic to the Indus River.

Therefore, most probably in 2002, The U.S. State Department took the initiative of funding the program called "The Pan Sahel Initiative" to help Mali, Mauritania, Niger and Chad protect their borders, monitor the movement of suspicious individuals, fight terrorism, and improve regional cooperation, peace and stability. Special forces of the U.S. Army, assigned to special operations under European Command (Special Operations Command Europe or SOCEUR), train military units of Mali and Mauritania. The SOCEUR forces, known for their ability to operate effectively in the roughest of environments, also benefit from this experiment to learn new cultures and terrains by working with African forces.

One of the successes of this program is probably the capture of Abderrazak Al-Para, a central figure in the Salafist Group for Preaching and Combat (SGPC), handed over to the Algerian government in 2004. But in spite of this success, the Pan Sahel Initiative found itself limited due to the level of funds committed and the objectives targeted.

Even though "Operation Enduring Freedom Chad" was independent of the Pan Sahel Initiative, its importance must be emphasized.

American counter terrorist commitments in the Sahel appear to have been respected in March 2004 through this operation to support the army of Chad in its armed combats against the SGPC. It appears that this battle first began in Niger before spreading to Chad.

In 2003, the United States European Command or EUCOM set up the "Joint Task Force Aztec Silence" that pursues the same counter terrorist objectives in North Africa where the governments of the contiguous States are, to say the least, fragile. Basically, it appears to be focused on the monitoring of these zones, the gathering of information and sharing it with the competent intelligence services of the relevant African countries. This American commitment is a clear message that the United States attaches increasingly greater attention to Africa as the next front in the global war on terror. They also seem to believe that it would be preferable to make modest short-term investments today to counter future problems requiring massive and costly American intervention.

In 2005, another extensive and larger operation was launched. This was the Trans-Sahara Counter-Terrorism Initiative. This new initiative was designed and planned as a logical continuation of the "Pan Sahel Initiative", which ended in early 2004. Apart from the countries directly concerned by the "Pan Sahel Initiative" (Mali, Mauritania, Niger and Chad), the new initiative concerns three North African countries (Morocco, Algeria, Tunisia) and three other African countries (Senegal, Ghana, and Nigeria), with Libya scheduled to participate later in this programme provided relations improve with the United States.

As the Sahel is a vast under-populated region, where there is little strict control by central governments, where borders are particularly porous and where war, sickness and poverty predominate, it was to be expected that terrorist groups would be particularly attracted to it. Traditional caravan routes are being transformed into weapons caches and training camps. The intelligence services of the U.S. Government have information about extremist groups with long experience in Afghanistan and Iraq which are operating in the Sahel. This is true of the Salafist Group for Predication and Combat that held 32 European hostages in 2003. These services also point to the existence of trafficking of arms, drugs and human beings whose desire to emigrate is exploited by this group. This new initiative is a central objective of the EUCOM strategic plan. The programme is believed to receive nearly one hundred million dollars annually, over a period of five years. In addition, it will benefit from the support of other bodies such as USAID for educational programmes, from the State and Treasury Departments, to improve controls on cross-border financial transactions, and from the competent authorities for airport security. The objective is to get the countries of the region to work together in terms of mutual security. The military aspect of the "Trans-Sahara Counter-Terrorism Initiative" is the "Enduring Freedom—Trans-Sahara" operation.

It would probably be wrong to believe that such threats are directed solely against the United States and African countries. Europe itself is concerned for reasons of external security without which no internal security is possible. Spain was hit by terrorist attacks in March 2004 in the suburbs of Madrid, claiming nearly 200 dead and 1500 wounded.

The same groups also hit the United Kingdom, in spite of the fact that the perpetrators of the terrorist strikes occurring in July 2005 in London, claiming 56 dead and over 700 wounded, were British subjects. Unable to understand and even less to explain this tragedy, an eminent member of the *Shadow Cabinet* kept on reminding us that "they are British, educated in our schools, and play cricket!!!". In his eyes, it would have been easier to understand if the perpetrators had been foreigners. The anger was obvious, but the astonishment, I suggested to him, had to do with a cultural explanation which here, as elsewhere, is mistaken. However, he remained doubtful.

Also to be noted is the rapprochement between the European vision of security and that of the United States even if the style may differ. Multilateral cooperation on security issues in the western Mediterranean initiated by France with the six so-called "format 5 + 5" countries, had the objective of establishing an action plan for maritime surveillance, civil protection and security in the air. The ten signatory countries were Spain, France, Italy, Malta and Portugal, and the five countries of the Arab Maghreb Union—Algeria, Libya, Morocco and Tunisia. Apart from the "security and defense" initiative, other tools for cooperation exist that it would not be appropriate to discuss in detail here.[1]

In fact, to different degrees, all countries are concerned by the threat of terrorism, a growing strategic threat, the proliferation of nuclear, chemical and bacteriological weapons of mass destruction, the spread of which among these groups is unknown, organized crime whose instigators and beneficiaries are ready to link up with terrorist groups, regional conflicts whose near or distant consequences affect the security of other nations, and the disintegration of States that some theorists of ethnicity and tribalism suggest as a solution to what they consider to be the failure of conventional state structures.

In a text with overtones of Tocqueville, and very forward thinking, given that it was published in 1957, Raymond Aron admirably expresses the very essence of terrorism when he writes: "Even if wealthy peoples are protected from invasion by weapons of mass destruction, they are not so from guerilla warfare. Guerrilla wars in our time have modified the map of the planet more than conventional or atomic weapons of mass destruction. A minority with strong resolve can make the lives of a dominant class unbearable once the ordinary people become more or less sympathetic to their aims. The cost of a counter-terrorism struggle rapidly becomes prohibitive for industrial countries with democratic regimes. Guerrilla warfare ended the European overseas Empires. Will it stop once anti-colonialism triumphs? Will the governments of liberated nations end the reign of violence they instituted to push out the conquerors? It is to be feared that a return to the rule of law is not yet imminent ..."

It is rightly said that contemporary terrorism is characterized by de-territorialization. It originates from no particular country and is global. New information and communication technologies play a decisive role in this de-territorialization. One can neither understand the extension of the Salafia Jihadia doctrine, born in the early 1960s, nor the powerlessness of the State confronted by the threats of this movement, if one forgets that the Internet assists in allowing the build up of a global network. This is demonstrated by preliminary investigations on the Jihadist websites by one of my students. This led to a thesis that, I hope, could be completed, amended and redefined according to sound theoretical assumptions.[2]

The power offered by the worldwide web to Jihadist leaders and the powerlessness of national States mutually feed into each other. Let me add that any attempt to create a sanctuary nation or continent is doomed to failure. No natural border, no wall, however high, can stop the spread of terrorist ideas and actions. Do we have a strategy for eradicating this evil? So far, there is nothing to suggest that we do. There is much hesitation, experimental solutions are put forth, stopgap measures are taken—all are obvious signs of the inadequacy of our diagnoses, in spite of the fact that our understanding of this phenomenon is improving.

It would be fastidious to draw up an exhaustive list of events occurring over the past few years proving that the Sahel is poised to become the preferred sanctuary of several terrorist groups. The American, Spanish, French, Moroccan and Algerian intelligence services all agree that the alarm bell should be sounded. Much research by experts in international relations testify to the presence of the SGPC, of Salafist or *Tablighis* groups, of activists of Islamist NGOs, the frequent contacts between them as well as certain segments of the Touareg tribes and the Polisario Front. The programmed implantation of Al Qaida in the countries of the Maghreb is no longer a secret to anyone. The events recently occurring in Algeria and Morocco are only the tip of the iceberg.

Even if there is no doubt that these organizations exist in the countries of the Sahel, it would be imprudent to assume the existence of a link between them and the many other Islamic movements in these nations. It would be even more dangerous to agree with the suggestion commonly proposed by certain governments, that political revolts and unrest are attributable to fundamentalist terrorist groups. Such hyperbole about the actual facts would lead to consequences contrary to those expected and would retroactively reinforce terrorism. It is known that terrorism leaves no stone unturned, and that it exploits misinterpretations of Islam. Therefore one must beware of any tendency to lump together different trends. The greatest danger would be to confuse the popular or informed practice of Islam existing in North Africa, the Sahel or even further in the Muslim world, and political fundamentalism that encourages activism and violence as solutions to global problems as perceived by certain active minorities.

Once again, convergence in the activities of the SGPC, its intensive recruitment among the Touaregs and the Polisario Front, the many types of polymorphous aid to all sorts of revolt, the numerous forms of trafficking, the activities of religious proselytes, in particular the *Tablighis*, deserve to be closely examined and permanently monitored. Some conclusions of the studies conducted by the International Crisis Group along these lines, appear to be justified and should be examined more closely.

It would also be imprudent to believe that there is a single solution applicable to all the countries of the region, as they are confronted by different social and political realities. Some are moving toward a democratization that is timid though real enough, and others are more fragile and dominated by ethnic groups whose dramatic consequences I shall attempt to discuss.

2/ TEMPTATION OF TRIBALISM AND DANGER OF RELATIVISM

It is no longer possible to deal with the problems in the countries of the Sahel and the Southern Mediterranean without discussing their economic, or more particularly, political problems. Indeed I have already discussed the significance of the economy for a country like Algeria. The political sphere appears to be even more important.

Several studies dealing with civil conflicts have attempted to identify the relationships between such conflicts and economic variables. It has been shown that poverty, economic recession and a dependency on natural resources are all risk factors explaining political instability. In fact, these studies spring directly or indirectly from the opportunity cost theory developed by Gary Becker (1968) and his students, principally Isaac Ehrlich (2006), to explain crime.[3] In outline this microeconomic approach to crime argues that criminals behave rationally in situations where the profits from their crimes exceed the costs of arrest and conviction.

It has also been suggested that one can explain violent behaviour and terrorism as a reaction to political conditions and frustration.[4] This theory suggests that economic factors do not determine political conflict or the established order in either a direct or simple manner. It is mainly after a period of rapid economic growth followed by recession, that creates frustration/deprivation for society members, that attempts at political unrest are most likely to occur.

Other explanations regarding violent commitment emphasize the axiological reasons for identity-driven membership of extremist groups. According to this theoretical perspective, ethnic or religious identities whose extremist versions are the so-called primordialist outlook, largely suffice to account for violent commitment.[5] In the latter instance, stress is put on the role of identities and analysis of the identity representations that can be conveyed within communities that make mobilization possible. These representations generally result from the work of those I have described elsewhere as proletaroid, ethnic or nationalist intellectuals who dwell on community "traditions", denounce the economic, social and political maginalization of their community and call for total war or separatism.[6] The discourse of these proletaroid intellectuals does not stop at building an image specific to their origin, they also try to create negative stereotypes used to single out anyone not belonging to their community attributing vices and hostile intentions to outsiders.

This theoretical diversity is an indication above all of the complexity of the problem and the difficulties that decision-makers have in developing effective public policy. Without the reduction of inequality without democratization of political life or without stabilization of all States, one would be led to expect growing instability and insecurity for all. The ethnocentricity and balkanization of the region, extolled by its advocates, do not bode well for international relations and the well being of peoples.

Concerning the region at issue here, it can be argued without much fear of error that to encourage greater ethnic identification and balkanization–both strategies for which some are ready to praise the potential benefits–are not likely to lead to a peaceful future in terms of international relations or the well-being of those concerned. Should the theorists of balkanization be reminded that many African leaders advocated a confederation just before the independence of West Africa? The idea, for instance, that French West Africa could be a single political entity was expressed in the 1950s by Léopold Sedar Senghor. In an article published in the December 1956 issue of *Afrique Nouvelle*, he argued forcefully against balkanisation of the ex-colonies. Today the question is whether the structures put in place by the then colonial power could have given birth to a federal State. It is known that things did not evolve in this way. It the book entitled *La balkanisation de l'AOF*, J-R de Benoist clearly shows how centrifugal forces finally won the day. After the rise of nationalism, the federal idea was taken up again by political and trade union leaders.

The balkanization of West Africa is the consequence of partisan calculation and political ambitions on a backdrop of economic covetousness. Even though the unitary project, completed in the late 19th century by the colonial power, served the designs of empire, it could also have become the framework for the emergence of future independent countries in the West African sub-region.

This attitude of colonial France was dictated by several motivations, in particular by the fact that the unitary claim, above all, was supported by those sectors most hostile to its presence, and that regional unity would eventually lead the emerging continent to escape its control. France supported those elements most subject to its influence, and the results of inter-African conflicts more often favoured those seeking a complete break.

Without a strong state, which does not necessarily rule out federalism, without democratization of the political sphere and greater social justice, without a correct interpretation of the values behind the thought and actions of certain elites and peoples, one must expect the rise of terrorist or mafia-like organizations. If they find at least passive support, their troops are likely to be recruited in sectors of society all too ready to listen to them. This is the assumption that underlies this part of my study devoted to the relationship between the state and the tribal tendencies within politics.

It would not be wrong to state that the collapse of the Soviet Empire is connected to the resurgence of nationalisms. Some nations became autonomous and quietly made the transition to a liberal economy and democracy. Others descended into extreme sectarianism, either ethnic or religious in nature.

It must also be added that globalization has reduced certain traditional spheres of state power and their management. This shows that many economic and financial decisions no long depend on the state, and are now dealt with by supranational institutions. In the economy, state intervention is decreasing on a daily basis and many sectors fall out of its control. It is no longer the master of its frontiers, or the markets it either opened or closed according to its own logic. Certain jobs and investments are becoming international. The European model of the welfare state is losing steam. In a nutshell, the state is reduced to its regal governmental functions. Globalization and fragmentation appear to be working together, administering a severe blow to it.

However, the state is a political form difficult to do without, at least for the moment. Its essential role is measured upon taking into consideration the negative consequences it engenders. It suffices to recall the recent examples of Yugoslavia, Liberia, Rwanda and Somalia. Almost all African countries—genuine ethnic mixtures—risk disintegrating into civil war and the increased reliance on ethnic and other identity resulting from the collapse of states. In the international context and openness to democratization can lead to the explosion of identity and sectarian tendencies, accompanied by violent rivalries. The case of Rwanda and Burundi, to mention only the most recent instances, are extreme examples. The ethnic group in Africa has rapidly become the foundation of political wheeler-dealing. Ethnic votes exist almost everywhere. In Africa, democracy is becoming hostage to tribalism.

Security is the origin of modern states. From Thomas Hobbes to Max Weber, political thought agrees on the idea that a social pact through which the citizen grants a share of his/her freedom to the

State so it can ensure security, social peace and equal justice to every-one, thereby suppressing the state of nature, overpowering rule by the strongest, and tyrannical power. It is in this spirit that one can under-stand the famous formula according to Weber that says that the state is defined by its monopoly over legitimate violence.

The weakening of States with the loss of control over their own territory, and the radicalization of the ensuing violence of terrorist groups against civilians, the means of destruction they could easily muster, constitute a great danger to international order.

From there originate two strategic necessities that no accountable state can readily neglect. Firstly, the state has the duty to intervene in all suspect areas likely to provide bases and logistic infrastructures supporting violent movements. Secondly, and related to the first neces-sity is that the international community has a right to interfere when human rights and universal values are seriously threatened, thereby making the principle of the sovereignty and intangibility of borders increasingly unjustifiable. It is in this new perspective that the issue of international security and globalization is posed from now on.

However, it must be immediately added that, following Max Weber and Raymond Boudon, I understand by universal values those that have historically proven their validity. A value can be considered as universal and irreversibly impose itself only if it is submitted to a series of tests that might take centuries to implement. But once recognized as such, they become irreversible. It is just that property which dis-tinguishes them from the traditions called into question as a result of negative experiences. This is also what distinguishes them from the particularistic values over which conflicts are inveterate, at the level of ideas and their ultimate logic, but that can be resolved by practical compromise.[7]

NOTES

1. I used information from the studies conducted by NATO researchers, the War School in France, information from the United States State Department and Department of Defense, and the reports of the International Crisis Group. There are so many that it would difficult to cite them all. On France's proposition see Coustillière (2005a, 2005b and 2006)
2. The thesis for the Advanced Study Degree entitled "The Djhaida Salafia network and its activity on the Internet" was prepared by Abdallah Rami.
3. See Collier (2000). According to him, a government is the custodian of national wealth and potential prey to "rebellious" predators who attempt to overthrow

it. The decision to act depends on the gains to be procured from violent action. The probability of action will be all the greater the higher the rewards. In other terms, the opportunity cost for putschists to overthrow the government will be higher when the country is poor.

4. The literature on frustration and deprivation is enormous and has existed for a long time as it goes back to Tocqueville (1853). Here, I will simply cite the work of Davies (1962), Gurr (1971), Krueger and Maleckova (2003). According to this theory, economic factors determine neither directly nor simply, political protest and changes to the established order. Generally, it is following strong economic growth followed by recession that attempts at political destabilization take place. See the critique by Coleman (1990).

5. See Brubaker *et al.* (2000, 2004)

6. I borrowed the expression "proletaroid intellectual" from Max Weber, see Cherkaoui (2006, 2007).

7. It is the theory of Max Weber that I discussed in Cherkaoui (2006), and which is brilliantly developed by Boudon (2004).

3

Morocco and its "Silent Revolution"

In the first part of this chapter, the reader will find a brief description of the political climate and institutional environment in which wide-scale autonomy for the Saharan regions has been proposed by Morocco. To understand this proposal and appreciate its true worth, it should be placed in a general context and global vision of the reforms that have been occurring in the Moroccan society throughout the last decade. It would be wrong to assume that this was simply an automatic process. Nor would it suffice to claim it was audacious, because to be accepted, it should be considered as the final step in self-analysis, analysis of the players involved and of Moroccan public opinion. It entails multiple political consequences. The constitutional changes required, the international commitments implied, the rights it grants to the Sahrawi people and the regional effects it risks by contagion—are perhaps the most important aspects.

In the second part, I will recall the historical and sociological factors bearing witness to the existence of strong links between the Sahrawi tribes and the Moroccan monarchy. One could interpret this according to the way one feels, one's vision of regional strategy, one's ethnocentric point of view or simply on regional and religious grounds. However, this would remain easy to question. I do not claim to offer a summary of the numerous and very learned studies conducted on this subject. It alone would require an entire publication of considerable

51

size. However, those studies do constitute the background to the second part of this chapter.[1]

1/ REFORMS

I will limit myself to the reforms made since July 1999, the date of accession to the throne of His Majesty King Mohammed VI. By seeking to compensate for the most substantial deficiencies impeding the Kingdom from becoming a legitimate state according to the most stringent international standards, by injecting a steady pace to institutional, economic and social change, the King courageously accepted some major risks. Promoting reforms is hardly an easy task. Often they give rise to political costs and sometimes unexpected consequences. "Such undertakings are not advisable. One can only accomplish them when one is sure of being able to ensure their proper establishment", to paraphrase a sentence by the author of *The Old Regime and the Revolution*.

The King's assurance seemingly resides in his belief in the soundness of an implicit theory of the evolution of modern societies, i.e. a theory whose principles can be deciphered through action, not words. This is explainable because of his dual religious and political legitimacy, the confidence of ordinary people evoked in national and international surveys of Moroccan public opinion, notably the *World Values Survey*. The data of this survey conducted by international experts obviously shows that the great majority of Moroccans trust the King more than any other person or institution. This is indicative of the obvious: the monarchy is the principal means for development and peaceful transition toward the practice of democracy in public life.

The Moroccan people have probably never before felt so free, with such a liberal press, though its excesses are sometimes only too evident. What militant could have imagined that one day the King himself would institute a genuine independent tribunal, the "Equity and Reconciliation Commission", enabling past infringements of human rights to be publicly judged, the responsibility of the state recognized and victims rehabilitated and indemnified? To immediately set aside any question concerning the independence of this tribunal, mention should be made that it consisted of former leftist activists, defenders of human rights, and was chaired by an ex-member of a Marxist-Leninist group and ex-political prisoner, enjoying full latitude to select counsellors among the most eminent law professors and lawyers. Its sessions were public. It travelled to parts of the Kingdom where witnesses could be gathered to speak about the violation of human rights.

By what standard was democratization measured between a Moroccan regime that made honourable amends and the oligarchy of a country that refused any inquest regarding the tens of thousands of disappeared persons, that even forbade seminars to be held on this topic, in spite of the fact the it signed the United Nations convention against forced disappearance?

Women benefit now from a more liberal family code, the devised through a process which involved all components of society. To do so, it was necessary to benefit from genuine religious legitimacy, demonstrate political courage and infinite patience to convince traditionalists, especially Islamic movements, of the need for such reform, that, let us recall, in March 2000 mobilized nearly two million demonstrators in Casablanca against a similar governmental project. Four years later, the new family code came into force. It was considered by *Global Rights*, an association for the defence of human rights in Washington, D.C., as one of the most progressive ever. It was a sign of the progress made with regard to the Moroccan woman. Henceforth, she can transmit her nationality to children resulting from a mixed marriage.

What other defender of the specific nature of Berber culture could have thought the language, poetry and traditions would be better preserved and expanded thanks to research generously funded by the public authorities, and also widely spread and taught in primary schools?

The King has overseen the application of social policy in its smallest details, in a bid to reduce inequalities and redistribute wealth, the effects of which are already being felt. The fight against homelessness, poverty in rural areas and exclusion in urban zones, thanks to training, vocational qualification, and the eradication of unsuitable housing through the building of new towns—all of these elements are the objective that the public authorities have been focusing on for two years by the provision of a fund involving several billion Dirhams.

A liberalization of the economy, and a vigorous thrust toward privatization of state-owned enterprises, coupled with political stability, has inspired foreign confidence and capital investment amounting to tens of billions of dollars, offering some obvious lessons to a hesitant local bourgeoisie.

It is true that the basic principles of such an economic policy are congruent with the dominant values in Moroccan public opinion which believe in the virtue of hard work, competition and the enterprise spirit, in the standards of a meritocracy justifying rewards that are proportional to the input, and to the advantages that it procures. Has not international comparative sociological research shown that in all these aspects, Moroccans appear to be more liberal, modern and better suited to accept the rules of a market economy than public opinion in European countries? It could be added that Moroccans, however, are more traditionalist with regard to religious values and norms in private life. The reader may refer to the voluminous and precise work carried out on the outlook for Moroccan society by 2030, conducted by the High Commission for Planning.

When, however, will we see the political parties respond to Royal admonishments asking them to be more open, to modernize the bureaucratic apparatus more quickly and to cease being the victims of the iron law imposed by a perverse oligarchy, and at last open up the political sphere?

This progress has been unanimously welcomed in the national and international press, to such a degree that *Der Spiegel*, spoke of the "*Friedliche Revolution*" ("pacific revolution"), and with regard to Morocco wondered whether the sought-after modernization, encouraged by His Majesty Mohammed VI, giving the example and precept, "*Wird es zum Modellstaat für einen demokratischen Islam?*" ("Will it become a model state for a democratic Islam?"). In order to illustrate these points, I have compared the performance of Morocco, Algeria with several other countries with a democratic tradition on the internationally recognised political terror scales. The reader will note the evidence of considerable progress in terms of the recognition of human rights in Morocco since the 1990s.[2]

In order to illustrate these points, I have compared the performance of Morocco with that of Algeria, and nations with a democratic tradition on the internationally recognised political terror scales. The reader will note the evidence of considerable progress in terms of the recognition of human rights in Morocco since the 1990s.

To fully appreciate these efforts, it must not be forgotten that Morocco has neither oil nor gas. Phosphates and their derivatives no longer constitute an important source of revenue. In reality, the sole resource on which the Kingdom can count is the human being. Producing high value added produce meant for export, developing the service sector in direct connection with international markets, injecting new momentum in the processing industry in compliance with international competition standards, and capitalizing on research and development require the real recognition and assessment of human capital and the work ethic. One indicator is telling: according to a study conducted by British Thomson Scientific on behalf of the Moroccan National Center for Scientific and Technical Research, Morocco comes 59th in the world for research in terms of quotations from scientific articles. A monumental study on human and social science research that I am on the verge of completing, led to very encouraging conclusions along the same lines.

And that is not all: Morocco is in the process of preparing other daring reforms. They will mean the delegation of powers to the major regions of the Kingdom that never enjoyed them in the past, even though they do currently benefit from a certain measure of freedom and prerogatives for transformation into genuine economic centres. In fact, reform began more than three decades ago when the communes became partially autonomous in managing community business. As of 1984, the late King Hassan II suggested the regions become true *Länder,* imitating Federal Germany by the end of an experiment they were to have initiated.

The national and international context, the outcome, assuredly hesitant, yet encouraging, of the decentralization experiment that has occurred in recent years, the attempt to draw public administration and the citizen more closely together, and make it more accountable for its decisions, the growing democratization of political life and a questioning of completely outdated practices, led His Majesty Mohammed VI to suggest new reforms.

2/ AUTONOMY OF THE SAHARA AND ITS INSTITUTIONAL FOUNDATIONS

The idea of reform also takes into consideration the difficult problem of the Sahara that calls for a solution acceptable to all parties as well as to the United Nations. As the two solutions envisaged, i.e. that of integration of the Sahara into Morocco, or of its independence as a result of a referendum, will not satisfy everyone, a third way was proposed. Kofi Annan and James Baker greeted it with interest. It consists of the integration of the Sahara into Morocco but with a wide degree of autonomy. As a matter of fact, it is possible to explain theoretically and practically why the idea of a referendum has no chance of being applied.

A project for a framework agreement was devised along the lines of this third alternative, suggesting a referendum in which all permanent residents of the Sahara would participate for one year prior to the vote. Morocco would be totally responsible for external relations, security and defense, "including determination of borders", the "preservation of territorial integrity against any attempt of secession", to which are added arms control, the currency, telecommunications, and customs, etc. (Framework agreement, par. 2). Therefore, to the Sahrawis would be handed the following responsibilities: local government, the budget, local taxation, internal security, culture, education, trade, transport, industry, etc. (Framework agreement, par. 2).

The project for extended autonomy of the Sahara that Morocco has just proposed to the United Nations Security Council, in the eyes of many international experts and observers, is the best solution setting aside strategic and regional issues, likely to satisfy the conditions enabling development of the well being of the local population.

Let us assume for the moment that the historical and religious arguments establishing the legitimacy of relations between the Sahrawi tribes and the King of Morocco, are being set aside. I will deal with unquestionable sociological factors, and consider the tribal structure and the environment which imposes its own laws.

The social and economic life of these tribes has never had specific territorial boundaries. Always on the move, between the Sous and the confines of the Anti Atlas, the Sahara, Algeria, Mauritania, Mali and Niger, they were not defined by any particular space, as was the case for the sedentary tribes of Morocco. Migrations were constant, and sometimes occurred in a space of several thousand kilometres. (See the trans-Saharan itineraries on the maps in the Appendix of Maps), which calls for no further comment). Such widespread dispersion was made necessary by the desert environment. Was it not written that the desert is subject to a fatal law, inherent to its very nature, according to which it always evolves toward the worst? The Sahrawis know this better than anyone else, and heed all the social and economic consequences. They also know that the Sahara had lived through progressive decadence of human life due to this implacable law in existence over the past centuries.

Sahrawi civilization never was and could never have been city-based. Agriculture and arboriculture were nigh on impossible, except in a few places where such activities were explainable more by reasons of prestige than by economic motives. Furthermore, working the soil was considered to be degrading and something to be left to the slaves. Oases were scarce and so poor that in 1950 it was exceptional to find any oasis with more than a thousand or so date palms. Apart from the plundering raids (*razzias*) that meant journeys of nearly 2,400 km, as was the case for the Rguibats in the winter of 1919–1920, and apart from the caravans bound for Marrakech, Senegal and the Atlantic coast, in those days called Sudan (Mali and Niger), hunting and nomadic pasturalism remained the sole activities, made necessary by the harsh living conditions. Even the Imraguen, mullet fishermen on the Atlantic coast, were frequently forced to resort to the nomadic life.

I will not dwell on collective behaviour, the regularly occurring tribal wars, the fluidity of social organization, the psychology, and relationships between men and women which can only be understood by the constant demographic imbalance between the two sexes, cultural output just as rich as anywhere else—all inevitably bearing the stamp of the desert. It is far from my aim to explain everything via functionalist theories. However, the Sahrawis have to confront problems posed by the environment to which they provide functional and rational responses.

Nothing distinguishes these tribes from the other Saharan populations of Mauritania, Algeria, Niger, Chad, Libya or Sudan. They all have the same culture, the same social structures, and the same way of life. This is not simply an ecological region called the Sahara, but rather, a genuine area of civilization. To define the natural, social and cultural frontiers of these populations, it would be necessary to take into consideration the entire space stretching from the Atlantic to the Red Sea and proceed to a new distribution of the countries involved. The irony of history is that the only country with legally and historically founded borders is Morocco, is called into question, while the other nations were delimited according to the desires of the coloniser and its relevant interests.

A firmly fixed territory was, therefore, an abstraction for the Sahrawis. To be fully convinced of this, all that is necessary is to consult the works of geographers, anthropologists or the invaluable report by the intelligence services of the British Admiralty produced after colonization by Spain and the French Protectorate in Morocco. Better still: the Spanish censuses of 1950 and 1970 indicate the presence of 85.6% and 70% nomads, respectively, in spite of the sedentary life made necessary by trading activities in cities during nearly one century of colonization. In this respect, let us summarize the great Sahrawi tribes and their zones of dispersion and economic interest.

Generally, the Sahrawi tribes are classified into four major groups, namely the Chorfa (nobles, presumed descendants of the Prophet Muhammad), Arabs, Tekna (almost all coming from the south of the Sous) and the Zenaga (Berbers originating from the region situated between Oued Draa and Jbel Bani). The Rguibats, Laaroussians, Oulad Bou Sbaas, Filalas, Taoubbalts, and Ahl Ma Al Ainains are all Chorfas. The Oulad Dlims, Chenagras, Escarnas are Arab tribes. The Ait Lahcens, Izerguiins, Ait Mousa Ou Alis, Yakouts, Ait Ousas all constitute the confederation of the Teknas. Oulad Tidrarins, Menasirs, Meyats, Lamyars, Fouikats, and Imraguens are Zenagas, or the descendants of the Zenagas.

I will not dwell on the details about the clans, divisions and infinite sub-divisions. Instead I will illustrate my observation by a few examples.

The Imraguens ("shell gatherers") constitute an industrious population. They lived in caves or huts on the southern side of the Sahara, but practised the nomadic life.

The Ahl Barakallahns, known for being the best camel breeders, formerly a liege tribe of Ma El Ainains, mainly lived in the deep South of Tiris and Inshiri, in other words, Mauritania.

The Tajakants or Jakanas, probably among the most numerous tribes, were sedentary, living in Ksour the main center being Tindouf, now in Algerian territory. This region was a part of the serious territorial dispute between Morocco and Algeria, and was handed over to Algiers only on the promise of economic cooperation that was to have been the first fruit and example of what the Arab Maghreb Union would have been.

The Izerguiins are a division of the Air Jmel branch of the great Tekna confederation. This tribe, like the Tekna confederation, was nomadic but its radius of action was limited to the basin of the Draa River and in the Nun.

The Aroussiyins, whose political and religious center was the mausoleum of Sidi Ahmed El Aroussi on the right bank of the river not far from Smara, were shepherds moving between the Draa and Saint Cyprian Bay. A part of this tribe emigrated to the region of Essaouira in a bid to escape dire poverty.

The Oulad Bou Sbaas, tribe whose camps were mainly in Mauritania, and also in the Haouz and Tazaroualat, the present-day region of Tiznit.

The Oulad Yahia Ben Otmanes, dominant in the 'Adrar et-Tmart, basically consisted of shepherds that grazed their herds in the basin of Draa and Draa and Adrar Souttouf.

The Rguibats, of the Sahel or from the west, and those of the Tell or the east, descendants of the Rif saint, Moulay Abdessalam Ben Machich, camel drivers and also occasionally farmers, camped out in Sakia El Hamra, but were shepherds stretching from Takna and as far as Mauritania.

The Oulad Dlims, shepherds and great warriors, were present throughout the entire Draa region, as far as Mauritania.

Therefore, it would be artificial to attempt to circumscribe these tribes within a territory assumed to be the Western Sahara, and to exclude them from the other immense Algerian and Mauritanian areas, that traditionally were part and parcel of the space in which they travelled.

However, a social link united all of them. It allowed them to transcend the confines of the tribe, that is to say, an allegiance they constantly demonstrated to the Moroccan Sovereign attaching them politically to the Kingdom of Morocco. The principle, let us recall, was recognized by the International Court of Justice which deemed that the Western Sahara never was *terra nullius*, even if it suggested an Eurocentric interpretation, different from that Muslim Law would give.

In this respect, it is dismaying to note a similarity between the exegesis of the Court and the declarations of Colonieu, a French army general in the colonial period, who either out of ignorance or cynical political calculation, argued that the links of allegiance by the Sahrawis with regard to the King of Morocco were strictly religious and that the King was only a sort of "Pope", as if one could separate the religious aspect of this allegiance from the political elements. Yet, one of the members of this high Court, judge Fouad Ammouni, a Lebanese Christian and excellent scholar of Islamic Law, spared no efforts in enlightening his eminent colleagues on the decisive political value of allegiance in the Muslim world. It was not deemed appropriate to take account of his observations.

A few words to enlighten the reader about the concept of allegiance (*Baï'a*) in Muslim Law may be useful here, even if the professional legal expert would probably not be likely to leave it at that. The *Baï'a* has only a distant relationship with the European concept of allegiance. In public law, it is a contract between the sovereign and the people. This contractual investiture is a rule for the organization of power renewed each year. In its extreme forms as recognized and accepted by the theoreticians of the said law, it sets limits on the sovereign and the political objectives for which he is accountable. Reference could be made to the section devoted to it by Ibn Khaldun in his *Prolegomena to Discourse on universal history* or to the first pages of *Governmental statutes* by Mawerdi.

Before colonization, Moroccan tribes, whether from the Sahara or not, were autonomous "republics" that the authority of the King joined together in a federal state, with the cement of allegiance. The expression "republic" was borrowed from Robert Montagne whom I consider to be the greatest anthropologist of the French school in the interwar period. His brilliant research on this subject is found in *Les berbères et le Makhzen au sud du Maroc/The Berbers and the Makhzen in the South of Morocco*. Sometimes the tribes formed coalitions in confederations or Leffs, as was the case of the Teknas.

For an instant, let us accept the principles of *Realpolitik* and assume that there is a desire to create a state uniting all the tribes of the Sahara. What would the consequences be?

Firstly, the Western Sahara is an immense desert-like territory of nearly 270,000 km², a population density far lower than one inhabitant per km² as the last Spanish census during the colonization period counted no more than 75,000 people, along the porous borders uncontrollable by a fragile state, dependent on foreign countries. The conditions favourable to the development of terrorist groups and clandestine immigration would converge. These destabilizing forces would threaten all these states, and to begin with, the Canary Islands.

Secondly, such an artificial creation would encourage claims already coming to a head, threatening the territorial integrity of other North African and Sahel states from the Atlantic Ocean to Sudan. In such a situation, Africa would be condemned to certain Balkanization with unimaginable consequences.

Should we doubt the resonance of tribalism in the social relationships within the Polisario Front? Without multiplying references on this subject, it suffices to quote written statements included in a recent book (Martinoli, 1998), *L'Ouest Saharien/The West Sahara*, which constitutes an apology for that organization: the "revolutionary project" (of the Polisario Front) has failed due to the "return of inequality in social relationships" (of the Polisario Front), in tribal solidarity, in dowries and in mistrust as experienced by young people returning from overseas, on the part of those who have stayed behind".

Increased autonomy in the Sahara would transcend historical logic; it would be a synthesis of the requirements of international law and *Realpolitik*; at the same time it would disqualify a tendentious interpretation of the principle of this right. It would guarantee the Sahrawi populations democratic self-management of community affairs while benefiting from the concessions Morocco has accepted and will continue to accept in spite of its limited resources.

This would offer a way out of the crisis providing an escape route for the Polisario Front that still refuses dialogue, whose decline is evident, as noted by several observers from a range of intellectual and political spheres. This has occurred in the form of the loss of former sources of funding, the waning of its radical socialist ideology, the dangerous slide into crime and closer ties to terrorist groups, the exodus of many well-to-do military and civilian Sahrawis from the camps in Tindouf toward Mauritania or the city of Zouerate, not to forget the many who have come to Morocco. Still more serious is the inability of the Polisario Front to continue to enlist young Sahrawis and, as a result, to renew its managerial staff.

A successful drive for autonomy is necessary for everyone. It will be a model for the other regions of Morocco. It will help further the democratization of Moroccan society and extend rights according to an irreversible process.

Today, Morocco is a centralized state. It lives under a legally centralized regime. Normative production is unified. All norms are applicable throughout the national territory. There is no constitutional or legislative autonomy even in an explicitly regulated form, and only very limited regional participation by indirect means through elected representatives. Regionalization, as it currently functions, does not exist in terms of the ability to produce or destroy norms. It is, rather a sort of administrative de-centralization.

To better envisage in the abstract possible options for the provinces of the Sahara and to identify the criteria of choice, internal decentralization of the Moroccan legal system must be taken into consideration before dealing with problems of centralization or decentralization that have an international dimension.

Let us examine international decentralization. Two options are possible: either decentralization concerns all regions or it concerns the Sahara only. In the first instance, all the regions benefit from the same resources and the system will be homogenous. In the second instance, the abilities of the Saharan region will be specific. The decentralization system will be heterogeneous or asymmetrical.

One can have a centralized and heterogeneous system like France because certain regions have laws different from those in force on the national territory or metropolis. On the other hand, the German, Austrian or Swiss system is homogenous, while decentralization is extensive. The Spanish and Italian systems are decentralized, yet homogeneous.

It appears that we are heading toward autonomy of the Saharan regions and for tailor-made abilities which the other regions will benefit from later on. In other terms, we accept temporarily an asymmetrical situation.

The values that autonomy brings will not fail to cross borders and spread in the countries of the region according to the mechanism of rational imitation or the domino effect model. It is founded on the theory of the evolution of modern societies which assumes that the only ones perceived to be legitimate are the institutions giving individuals a feeling of their dignity and the preservation of their vital interests.

The failure of this would put an end to the silent revolution Morocco is going through. It would call into question many national and international commitments and would lead us to a future full of uncertainty and perhaps even regional chaos.

Figure 3.1: *Comparison of values on the political terror scale between five countries (1980–2005): Morocco, Algeria, United States, France and the United Kingdom*

The following figures have been developed on the basis of data taken from "Facts on International Relations and Security Trends", which is a joint project of the "International Relations and Security Network" and the "Stockholm International Peace Research Institute".

The comparison per country pair shows a gap existing between Morocco and the other nations. To facilitate consultation, it was impossible to represent the chronicles on just one graph.

The scale of political terror varies from 1, the lowest level characterized by the rule of law, to 5 or highest level, where political terror is rife and spread throughout the population, where torture and imprisonment are frequent for political and ideological reasons, and where murder is commonplace.

For each country we have two assessments: the first is by Amnesty International, the second by the U.S. State Department. The U.S. State Department gives no assessment for the United States. Only one exists, i.e. by Amnesty International. Moreover, to stabilize the graph, we attributed the average grade for two adjacent years of the country and for the year when the information is absent. This is the case of the United Kingdom in 1996 and France in 1997, years when Amnesty provides no information on these countries.

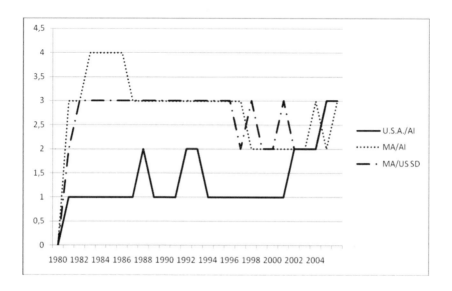

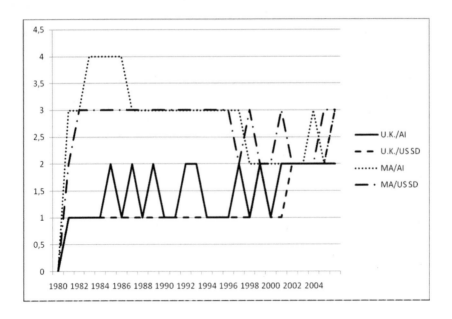

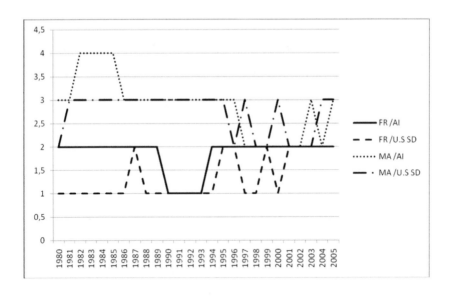

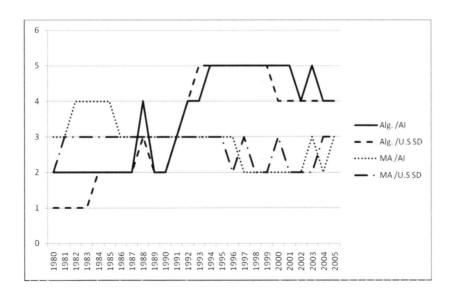

Generally, one finds strong congruence between the assessment of Amnesty International and the U.S. State Department. To be noted is that for Morocco, since the second half of the 1990s, the values fluctuate between 2 and 3. This is an obvious sign of a change with regard to human rights and the gradual move towards a legitimate state. For all countries of great democratic tradition like the United States, France and the United Kingdom, the values fluctuate between 1 and 2. Few are the countries for which the value of the political terror index remains constantly at 1, as is the case of Sweden.

The extreme values reported for Algeria, between 4 and 5, are to be correlated with the civil war in this country since the beginning of the 1990s, bearing witness to the most serious blows to human rights.

NOTES

1. We consulted, among others, publications of Naimi (2004), Briggs (1960), Institut des Hautes Etudes Marocaines (1930), Rezette (1975)
2. Refer to the graphs representing a comparison of value on the scale of political terror among five countries: Morocco, Algeria, United States, France and the United Kingdom.

Part Two
Social and Economic Integration of the Western Sahara

4

Integration and its Measurement

Surely, nothing can be reduced to sheer politics, or the most clever and Machiavellian sleight of hand. Nothing is settled by decree or abstract principles, even if universal in nature. However, the nobility of politics lies in its capacity to allow all populations to live together that are, in principle, heterogeneous. In so doing, along with other factors, this contributes to integration. To ignore it would be tantamount to a failure to understand the problem of nationalism or of relations with the state. No genuine political theory can neglect the issue of integration which lies at the heart of apparently dichotomous conceptual pairs, i.e. ethnic or cultural minorities–nationalism of the state with clearly defined borders, past–present, nationalism–universalism, community–society, and tradition–modernity, etc. Ernest Gellner, the anthropologist and also the theoretician of nationalism, and successor to Renan and Max Weber, fully understood this when he emphasized the strong bonds between the state and culture, turning away from primordialist theories for which nationalism constitutes an awakening and the blossoming of myths assumed to be natural and self-evident. The permanent plebiscite, so dear to Renan, as he so rightfully states, occurs every day and in conjunction with each start of the school year. In other words, the concept of the nation automatically refers indirectly back to the political.[1]

The following reflections and analyses deal with this issue for the Sahrawi population, and more generally for this great blend of tribes, of men and women all of different extraction from regions each with their specific character, who have accepted a joint destiny and define this historical singularity known as Morocco.

For the Sahrawis, what were the consequences of Morocco's recovery of its southern provinces? Has the Moroccan State practised a policy of development in this region? Has the general well-being of the population been improved? Or, on the contrary, has it stagnated or even become worse? Even if there has been some evolution, would it be possible to measure the growth rate and describe the trends in the most important and diversified spheres of activity?

Assuming that the response to these questions is positive, could we deduce this that the Sahrawi population is actually integrated into global society? Are there no other dimensions of integration that could also be analysed and measured?

To believe that integration is limited to an economic problem, possible to solve through massive investment, would be theoretically inadequate and practically dangerous. It would be tantamount to explaining it in crypto-Marxist terms, the theoretical bankruptcy of which is generally well-known. It also would be tantamount to making a fatal political mistake. Isaïah Berlin, along with many others, states, with reason, that one of the major failures of Marxism is of not being in a position to explain nationalism and religion as factors having specific autonomy and thus irreducible to the economic sphere and its own logic.[2] The political consequences of such a limited vision are devastating. To be convinced of this, all that is necessary is to open one's eyes to certain phenomena observable in most regions of world.

After all, some would rightly say that the improvement in living conditions of the Sahrawis has had no mechanical effect on the social integration of this population, no impact on Saharan social structures that remain autonomous, impermeable to any exogenous change and resistant to any interpenetration of "external" elements.

This argument is substantial. It deserves further consideration of its validity and force. If indeed, the Sahrawi tribes as well as those dwelling in other regions of Morocco, consisted of heterogeneous groups, two societies without common denominator, with two specific cultures, the consequences could be drawn from it. If, on the other hand, they consisted of only one society, organized according to local specificities, in the Sahara and elsewhere in Morocco, it would be humanly and politically a very grave matter to divide them into two entities foreign to each other.

By pushing the logic of the secessionists to its extreme limits, one would wind up with dismemberment of Morocco. This would apply to the Sahara and to any other region of the national territory. Each ethnic and linguistic group, each confederation of tribes, each fraction of tribe, would demand total autonomy and claim a state viable only in the morbid imagination of the sophists of cultural and social relativism. The postmodern theoreticians who pit the ethnic group against the state would obviously rejoice, but the consequences of their ideas would give rise to unfathomable damage.

1/ FIELDS OF STUDY

Without excluding from my analyses the various fields entering into this issue, I will emphasize education because it determines the future of the young generations and because I have relatively extensive data making it possible to describe models of change in school and university demography, and to predict what is in store in the medium and long terms.

How has the level of education of the Sahrawis changed since 1975? Has inequality between males and females become worse or has it been drastically reduced? Are these changes identical to those occurring in other regions of the Kingdom, or have the Saharan provinces seen change specific to them? If that is the case, have they been discriminated against, or on the contrary, have they been favoured in comparison to the other regions of Morocco? In sum, it would be of the greatest and even vital interest to test the assumption that the Moroccan authorities may have applied to the Sahara a policy of positive discrimination, in face of the extreme poverty which the Sahrawis experienced in times of colonization. This also would involve measuring the effects. The policy of positive discrimination by the Moroccan State since 1975 would consist of a series of measures devised and applied to correct past negative discrimination and the inequality thereby engendered.

Take the case of illiteracy. We all know it has fallen. But it would be both instructive and useful to determine the model of evolution over several years. Does the drop in illiteracy follow a linear model or is it more like an exponential model? Indeed, both are indicative of the decline in this phenomenon. However, they do not express the same degree of intensity and do not tell the same story. The first corresponds to a single public policy consistent over time, without any global effect. The second represents either an intensification of government measures designed to eradicate the global effect of this evil, or cumulative effects.

The identification of the most adequate model for describing reality is not only of theoretical interest, the importance of which for the researcher is easy to understand. It also offers practical perspectives because it enables the decision-maker to measure the consequence of his/her former educational policy and to specify the means he/she expects to implement and the time frame reasonable to propose.

The general assumption that the present study will attempt to test is that, confronted with the scarcity and poverty the Sahrawis were facing in 1975, for the past three decades Morocco has devised and applied a policy of positive discrimination, transfer and support by the state in fields as varied as education, health, housing, infrastructures, direct state intervention on the job market giving priority to Sahrawis for employment, to the extent in which they could enter into equitable competition with other citizens who benefited from advantages in the past, etc.

To be strict, one can verify the soundness of this assumption in all fields. However, here I shall limit myself to education, housing and human development, as well as to certain infrastructures as the data available do not make it possible to strictly test this assumption in all its scope.

Other issues deserve to be looked at, and other assumptions would benefit from being tested. However, it would not be possible to go beyond what such data allow us to do.

2/ DIMENSIONS, INDICATORS AND MEASUREMENT OF THE CONCEPT OF INTEGRATION

Should I discuss integration in sociological and political terms, once the previously formulated assumption has been tested? Do the Sahrawis feel objectively integrated into global Moroccan society?

Here, by integration, I understand not in terms of the positive consequences of public policy, but rather, in terms of the force of the *social bond* between the components of a general whole. The social bond is first and foremost a structural property of all social groups, whether domestic, religious, political or economic. Provisionally, I will define it by the volume, extension, intensity and density of the reciprocal social relationships that the Sahrawis entertain with other Moroccans.

Successful integration means that the social bonds between individuals and groups belonging to these populations and other Moroccans are so strong that a break up would disorganize society as a whole. It implies that these units henceforth make up a part of one and the same community, and therefore of the same nation. So long as these conditions are not met and whatever the achievements of the central state or its representatives in this region, it would be risky to speak of sociological integration. The opposite of integration is exclusion, fragmentation, the development of social ghettos or even apartheid, even in a benign form.

From a sociological point of view, integration is a multidimensional concept.[3] The first dimension of its theoretical space is morphological or structural. The indicators of this dimension are multiple. They extend from relationships of good neighbourliness, social and geographical mobility, frequent interchange, and contacts that the members of society entertain with others. They can be empirically measured by indices of interdependence between the individual and groups that may vary from total independence, in other words from weak or non existent social bonds, to social communion, an extremely rare case occurring only in certain circumstances, for example, with respect to religious experiences.

The market is the topical example of exchange. If individuals consider exchange not as a zero-sum game, where the gain of one agent of the transaction is equal to the loss of the other, but rather as cooperation game, and if they deem the contribution to the transaction is beneficial to everyone, it could be said that they accept the common rules of the game and that they are not in an anomic society where everyone wages a war against the other. In a nutshell, cooperation is a fundamental component of the exchange.

Let us say from the outset, cooperation is not the result of regulations imposed from the top, even if by a well-meaning regime, or from the outside, by an international organization, but, rather a consequence sought by individuals and generated by units in the social system itself. Among the indicators of this cooperation, we can cite the investments made by Sahrawis in other regions of Morocco, in the Sahara or investments by non Sahrawis who have been willing to move capital and labour to the Sahara since 1975. If I had had systematic statistical data on such investments in both directions, I would have been in a position to establish these facts. In Morocco, as in France or other countries, the gathering of statistical information is never based on ethnic or religious criteria. The information I have in support of this thesis is unfortunately incomplete. It does not make it possible to conduct a demonstration as rigorously as I would have liked.

To take into consideration the specific nature of Sahrawi tribal social structure, the growth in heterogamous marriage is the best indicator of this dimension.[4] Actually, in segmented societies like traditional Sahrawi society, the rules presiding over the choice of a spouse are almost intangible. Except for exceptional and sometimes codified instances, no one can normally fail to respect the rule imposed on a man to take as spouse the woman of another tribe or to marry his parallel cousin, the daughter of a father's brother (*bint al-'amm*), which is commonly referred to by the Arabs as preferential marriage. In this type of society, belonging and integration into the different social orders is based on blood relationships and marriage. Empirically establishing that marriages in the Sahara are becoming increasingly heterogamous, is tantamount to recognizing that the populations making up this region are integrating into global Moroccan society.

However, one observation should be made. Strictly speaking, to measure the heterogamous nature of marriage, it does not suffice to simply analyse the evolution of this phenomenon in the Saharan regions. It is also necessary to place it in the more general framework of Moroccan society which itself is characterized by a very high rate of social, local and tribal homogamy. In Morocco endogamous marriage, whether territorial or social, is very frequent. However, it is noteworthy that such social homogamy relaxes somewhat as society changes and modernizes. Emile Durkheim, the founding father of French sociology, would have doubtlessly seen in this phenomenon, proof of passage from a society of mechanical solidarity to one of organic solidarity. Formerly, marriage between a woman from Fez, Rabat, Tetouan or Berber speaking provinces and a partner from another region was extremely rare, even if they hailed from the same socio-economic milieu and even if the fiancé was from a higher social stratum than his future spouse. Such unions are a bit more frequent today. A study on the choice of the spouse in Casablanca I conducted twenty years ago, showed that the rate of social endogamy remains very high, in spite of the fact that the large metropolis is a relatively open place where blending of populations is much greater than anywhere else in Morocco.[5]

A study of this phenomenon in the Sahara should follow the same methodology, taking into account the same remarks and respect of local specificities. To understand the considerable scope of heterogamous marriage among this population, figures are not sufficient in that they remain silent on its meaning and the sociological significance. To be taken into consideration is the force of tribal bonds which partially prohibit heterogamy. Also to be kept in mind are the demanding material conditions required for the union. In the Sahara more than in other regions of Morocco, marriage is a demonstration of the financial status of the families, of generosity, and power. It implicates too many people. Economically ruinous, the ostentatious consumption, the gifts and gifts in return required by a marriage are so considerable that the non-Sahrawi would find it difficult to fathom.

The reader will, therefore, understand that the wager I have made is very risky. It is infinitely easier to lose than to win. But my conclusion will have to be accepted if ever I detect the slightest premise for these unions in a milieu that finds it hard to accept.

Morphological integration applies to individual relationships and global society. The first could be described as social or structural, and the second systemic.[6]

The second dimension of integration is of a normative order. It signifies that individuals share common values and norms, the same beliefs and same practices expressed and more or less materialized, to form a "collective conscience". This normative dimension is generally engendered by socialization processes that are deployed and reveal their polymorphous effects over time. This also applies to religious beliefs and practices.

I hasten to add that integration does not assume identical forms of behaviour but, rather, their convergence and coherence. Invariance is not a characteristic of human behaviour. As normative as things may be, any action assumes departures from the norms as understood here in both the statistical and axiological sense.[7]

The third dimension is of a prospective order. By this we understand the fact that individuals feel dedicated to common ends. The most important indicators of this dimension are of a political order, but not exclusively so. Individuals take as an objective a common future, whether political, cultural or social. A similar perception of the future, however, does not exclude confrontation or conflict. The members of a society can aim at the institutionalization of a democratic society, for example, by taking routes to it that may sometimes be different.

In fact, good integration does not mean the total absence of conflict. Paradoxically, conflict does not exist between foreigners. No sign of it is detected including between neighbours who do not know each other or, better yet, who exchange nothing more than gestures of courtesy when they happen to meet. Much sociological research demonstrates, contrary to what is thought, that conflict is a part of integration. In traditional Moroccan society and in Sahrawi social structures, conflicts between segments or between tribes and the central authorities are frequent, even though no one really questions the legitimacy of global social order that integrates units of the sociopolitical system.[8]

Thus, paradoxically, contrary to an ordinary and superficial reading more oriented to the sensational and spectacular than to comprehension, demonstrations by young Sahrawis might be interpreted, according to us, as a good indicator of systemic integration to the extent in which it expresses a wish for the State to handle of their social and economic problems. Rather than considering them as expressions of rejection, of revolt or as being irrational or sporadic, they could be interpreted as being the consequence of inter-generational conflicts, between older people who were the recipients of substantial economic aid and younger people who compare themselves to the older generations and feel they do not enjoy the same advantages as their elders. That is a topical example of the phenomenon of relative deprivation that sociological theory is in a position to explain.

It is not necessary to build imaginary theoretical hypotheses such as the theory of manipulation or conspiracy, to explain these social movements. It suffices to analyse the situation on the job market and its consequences for the lives of young Sahrawis or non-Sahrawis to explain protest movements.

For those hankering for the sensational, desperately seeking to impress pubic opinion by provocative headlines on the front pages of weeklies, I am reminded that the same events occurred in regions neighbouring the Sahara and in the North of Morocco proving that they are not specific to young Sahrawis. They do not care a whit about the Tenka and other populations of the Draa, Ifni or elsewhere.

The indicators of political integration are many indeed. This is true of the people fleeing the camps of Tindouf in Algeria and returning definitively to Morocco, of the many political personalities who appear on the front pages of newspapers, the rate of registration for elections, and the participation of Sahrawis in local and national elections.

So if such integration occurs, it would be difficult, or even impossible, to separate the populations into two entities without simultaneously creating human tragedies. Would one want to see fathers and mothers living separately in two distinct states? How could one explain to children that they have to choose to live with one or other of their parents? Would one resort to throwing dice to split them up? They would pay no attention to the Machiavellian calculations of the powerful of this world, to the legal principles applied. No principle is legitimate if it does not respect the dignity of human beings and their right to live according to the path they have traced for themselves. Its legality would be of little importance, even were it to be international.

3/ AVAILABLE STATISTICS, DATA TO BE CONSTRUCTED AND PROBLEMS OF METHOD

Gathering data is not an easy task. Statistics concerning the populations I am studying here are widely scattered. Some of the data is available, other data relative to education, demography, elections, poverty and human and social development indicators, have to be collected and compiled. Studies by the High Commission for Planning, conducted according to the international standards of the International Monetary Fund will be widely used.

Other data do not exist. This is the case for marriages. The data have to be constructed based on a systematic analysis of official registers containing marriage licenses. There are over 200 registers from the 1970s to 2006. The number of marriages must be near to 30,000. Drawn up by *Adouls*, or legal clerks, these contracts are handwritten. The information contained therein has to be translated and encoded in digital form so they can be analysed by adequate software. The data are the only ones that are at an individual level. Therefore, they pose no particular problem with respect to method.

Other statistics, on the other hand, consist of aggregate data found at the level of the commune. This relatively high level of aggregation gives rise to methodological problems recalled very briefly here.

The objective of analysis of the data for the last three Moroccan population censuses of 1982, 1995 and 2004—is to present a synthesis of the evolution of the most important sociological and economic indicators concerning the situation in the Saharan provinces. This does not only mean describing the real situation, but rather, answering the questions pursuant to both the absolute and relative improvement in the living conditions of individuals residing in these region since the end of Spanish colonization in 1975 and to 2004, the date of the last Moroccan census. For this purpose, I will refer to all the data from the Spanish censuses of 1950 and 1970 available in the *Fondo Documental del Instituto Nacional Estadistico* for the two years I am concerned with. In that way I have a series of continuous statistics dealing with at least a half a century. However, I regret that certain data on the Sahrawi population do not exist: the Spanish demographers paid little attention to their then colony, as compared to Sebta and Melillia for which the same data were collected as for the rest of Spain.

I cannot end this brief introduction without saying something about the major methodological problem arising from this data. The observation units being the communes, I cannot generalize the propositions that my analyses make possible and directly apply them at the individual level. Indeed, it is sometimes erroneous to deduce, without additional hypotheses, individual behaviour or its status based on the behaviour of ecological units such as the communes. Inferences about the individual based on the collective is what is describes as the contextual fallacy, and is well known, especially in electoral sociology.

NOTES

1. The remarks on the relationship between the state and nationalism on one hand, and integration, on the other hand, are cursive and to my mind no more than a brief description of one aspect of sociological and political theories affecting closely or at a distance, the issue concerning us here. I implicitly refer to the reflections of Ernest Renan developed in his essay entitled *What is a nation?*, and the section entitled *"Die Nation"* of *Wirtschaft und Gesellschaft*, and other essays of Max Weber *Die Nationalstaat und die Volkswirtschaftspolitik, Parlament und Regierung im neugeordneten Deutschland, Wahlrecht und Demokratie in Deutschland*. Weber's idea of the national foregoes any ethnic or linguistic foundation. It deals with joint destiny and its relation to the state or the ideal power, to the extent in which, as opposed to joint destiny and its relationship with the state, unlike to the idea of Renan, exclusively oriented toward internal politics, he deems that it necessarily encompasses external policies. A nation without a strong state, incapable of playing the slightest role in the equilibrium of regional forces, over time, is finished. Weber, however, underlined the moderation the central state should demonstrate with regard to its ethnic and cultural minorities. The German sociologist defended this point of view in the case of the Poles of Prussia. To my knowledge, the best presentation of this aspect of Weber's theory is by Mommsen (1959).

   The thesis of Weber strongly influenced his followers, like Edward Shils (1957, 1995), Karl Deutsch (1969), Anthony Smith (1992), and Walter Connor (1994), even though some defended the primordialist thesis and more greatly under-scored the primacy of ethnicity over integration. Gellner (1983), an orthodox follower of Weber, was on the other side from the primordialists.

2. For an analysis of the failure of Marxist theory, see Berlin (1973),

3. With regard to integration the reader will have understood that I refer principally but not exclusively, to the theory of Emile Durkheim (1895, 1897, 1912). Integration is not a recent problem in social science. One can go all the way back to the *Leviathan* of Hobbes. The Scottish philosophers, in particular Adam Smith and David Hume, dealt with this concept according to several points of view: that of cooperation and interchange on the market. The works of Homans (1974), Blau (1964), Harsany (1968), Axelrod (1984), and Coleman (1990) continue the methodological individualist paradigm. These theoreticians of rational choice speak of cooperation in terms of maximization of the utility of the players concerned.

The issue of integration is also at the heart of the *Social Contract* of Rousseau and Saint Simon on which Durkheim (1900) piles endless praise by qualifying it as a "new Christopher Columbus" for having discovered the crucial importance of the idea of interdependence. Durkheim's theory, to me, seems more complete and doubtlessly explains it better than does the purely utilitarian traditions, to the extent in which it takes into consideration the axiological aspects of integration, as does Max Weber. In fact, functionalist theories like those of Durkheim and Parsons (1950) play on two utilitarian and normative planes.

The three dimensions of integration, morphological, normative and prospective that we distinguish here, are taken from the theory of Durkheim I put forward in Cherkaoui (1998).

4. Taking marriage as a central indicator of integration is an idea common to several anthropological and sociological studies that cannot all be mentioned here. Let it suffice to say that reference can be made to the remarkable work of Peter Blau (1977, 1984). His macro-structural theory and that of the networks shed light on the issue of the social bond, based on two points of view: the first is macro-sociological, and the second micro-sociological.

5. The study on the choice of spouse in Casablanca, showed that the rate of pure endogamy reaches almost 20%. Preferential endogamous marriage varies depending on the level of education and age, reaches 40%. The rate of homochtony—regional or geographical homogamy—sometimes reaches 80%. That is to say that in a city like Casablanca, which is a social melting pot and symbol of modernity, heterogamy is rare. It goes without saying that the rates of endogamy and homogamy are thought to reach higher levels in medium size cities and in rural areas.

6. I take the distinction between social integration and systemic integration from Lockwood (1964).

7. The idea of behavioural norms in the statistical and normative meaning of the term can also be found in Durkheim and Nadel (1970).

8. Here I refer to the theory of conflict of Simmel (1908), the fecund nature of which was shown by Coser (1956). The conflicting relations between tribes and the Moroccan monarchy are extensively documented. Well before the anthropologists, Moroccan historiographers drew attention to one of them. One of the

best anthropological studies remains that of Montagne (1930). Many notes on the same phenomenon can be found in the anthropological research on tribes in Morocco, in particular, Berque, Hardt, Eickelman. It would be impossible to mention them all. Reference should be made to Gellner (1969), and Hammoudi (1974, 1980).

5
Declining Illiteracy

It would seem logical to begin by asking about the role that has been and is still played by the most important agent of socialization and integration for different generations, in a nutshell, the school. It is within this institution that future generations are scientifically and culturally formed. In addition, it is known that the educational system plays a major role in modern societies insofar as it is the Archimedean point of any economy focusing on the increasingly predominant tertiary sector, based on continuous innovation and scientific research, requiring highly skilled labour.

In this chapter, I will analyse the evolution of illiteracy and the progress made in schooling by the Sahrawi people, and proceed to an explanation thereof, data permitting. No one would be surprised if I take as the date of departure of our longitudinal analyses, the year 1975, corresponding to the last days of Spanish colonization. I will use the rare and oldest Spanish data whenever available and whatever its validity and precision, for after all, it is preferable to have sketchy information rather than none whatsoever.

The purpose of this study is to gauge the impact of education policy in the Sahara since that date. To evaluate the policy of positive discrimination regarding the Sahrawis, I will compare the results obtained by the population this region, with schooling in other regions of Morocco chosen according to their geographical and social proximity to the Sahara. However, this will not hinder us from comparing it to the data on the most highly developed region of Morocco, namely Greater Casablanca.

1/ FALLING TRENDS IN ILLITERACY

To maintain readability of the text, I refer to the appendix with tables representing the results of analysis of the data originating from three censuses. They permit me to formulate the following proposals.

1/ In 1982, the global rate of illiteracy in the Saharan provinces was very high, reaching approximately 70%, with nearly 55% for males and 84% for females. As there are no valid statistics for the colonial period, one can only assume that these rates reached all-time peaks largely exceeding those of the general Moroccan population census of 1982. If the Spanish data is to be trusted in the *Fondo Documental del Institut Nacional de Estadistico* of 1970, the rate of illiteracy of the Sahrawi people hovered around 94%. This result is not really surprising when considering that at the time of independence of Morocco in 1956, schooling in the Northern zone under Spanish Protectorate had a very high rate of illiteracy. Other sources show that in 1975, the Sahrawis had not even one secondary educational institution.

2/ The distribution of illiteracy for both genders is highly unequal from one region to another and one milieu to the next.

3/ In the course of each decade, the illiteracy rate fell by 10 points, dropping from 55 % in 1982 to 45.2% in 1994 and 34% in 2004, for males from 84%, to 73% and for females to 56.3%, respectively. Females showed the highest rate in the reduction of illiteracy. We can illustrate in graph form the drop from 1982 to 2004. The following figures demonstrate the constantly falling drop in illiteracy and its negative growth rate. This drop and its intensity are higher for females than for males, as the difference between the rate for both genders falls from one decade to another. In 1982, this difference was of almost 39% (83.7%–55%); in 2004, it was of only 22% (56.3%–34%). As an initial approximation, if we adjust the simplest model, i.e. that of a regression line, with respect to empirical data, it can be seen that the slope for females is higher than for males. Moreover, one can predict that, all other things

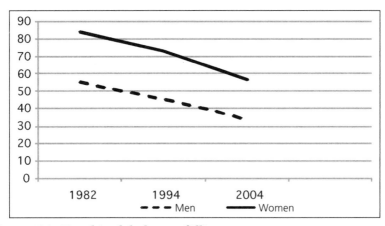

Figure 5.1: *Trend in global rate of illiteracy*

being equal, if this trend continues, the inequality between males and females will disappear by 2020.

4/ Also to be noted is that the degree of regional inequality, as measured by variance, tends to show a slight drop, i.e. indicative of the relative efficiency of educational policies geared towards reducing regional disparities.

5/ If a global comparison is made between the illiteracy rate in the Sahara and that of the rest of Morocco, there is no significant difference except for Sahrawi females for whom the rate is slightly less high than the national average (56 vs. 57%).

6/ Examination of the evolution in the values of skewness in the distribution of illiteracy rates for the three points of observation, lend ample backing to these propositions. These values evolved from 0.34 in 1982 to 2.3 in 2004 for males, and from 0.41 to 1.13 for females. The interpretation of these values is immediate. We move from distributions of illiteracy almost according to a normal law, to strongly asymmetrical distributions to the right, showing a drastic reduction in illiteracy rates. This phenomenon can also be detected in the values of modes and medians, reduced by half, in the first instance moving from 40 to 21 for males and from 74.4 to 53 for females, and for the second from 56.4 to 25 for males, and 83 to 46.5 for females.

7/ However, to obtain a precise idea of illiteracy in the Saharan regions, and measure the degree of regional inequality, one must take into consideration the social make-up. One must compare the rate of literacy in the Saharan provinces to similar regions.

2/ COMPARISON BETWEEN THE SAHARAN AND NON SAHARAN REGIONS

Let us begin by stating that the illiteracy rate in Laayoune-Boujdour (LB), a region with high urban concentration, offering more school places than elsewhere in the Sahara, is less than in the other Saharan regions i.e., Guelmim-Es-Smara (GS) and Oued Ed-Dahab-Lagouira (OL).

1/ Laayoune-Boujdour in particular registers a remarkable drop approaching the lowest rate of illiteracy in the best performing regions of Morocco. In addition, illiteracy has dropped to such a degree that it is the lowest compared to the rate in four other and most similar regions, namely, Chichaoua, Taroudant, Sous-Massa, and Figuig. Only Greater Casablanca registered a lower rate. This is not surprising as Greater Casablanca is the most dynamic region of the Kingdom for employment, having high density in processing and service industries, with strong cultural capital and generator of the largest revenues.

2/ These findings apply to rural zones. Once again, only Greater Casablanca reports a lower rate than the Saharan provinces.

Table 5.1: *Rate of illiteracy according to gender, region and residential area*

Urban

	LB	GS	OL
Male	20.0	21.2	24.9
Female	38.8	45.1	45.1
Total	29.0	33.4	34.0

Rural

	LB	GS	OL
Male	33.9	33.6	62.8
Female	53.2	66.2	38.6
Total	41.8	52.2	57.3

3/ It is noteworthy that the inequalities between males and females are almost identical for all the regions investigated. The illiteracy rate for females is almost twice as high as that of males in urban zones and slightly less so in rural zones. The only exception, however, is to be pointed out, namely Oued Ed-Dahab-Lagouira in rural areas where, curiously enough, the illiteracy rate for women is much lower than that of men.

4/ In this proposal one would be mistaken to decipher a paradox and deduce that the conclusion that inequality according to sex is higher in urban than in rural milieus. In fact, this paradox is explained by the mode of calculation adopted, that is to say, the percentage ratios. It disappears when the analysis is based on the difference between percentages. In the latter instance, one remarks the same gap between males and females in both rural and urban environments is seen. The gap between the sexes is approximately equal to 30% for all regions and milieus.

5/ Several lessons can be learnt from the analysis of the rate of illiteracy distribution.

Firstly, there is an evident reduction in inequality measured by variance. This is true for males and females. However, the inequality between females is greater that between males.

Table 5.2: *Illiteracy rates in five regions of Morocco according to gender and residential area*

Urban

	1	2	3	4	5
Male	25.0	22.8	20.6	20.3	14.9
Female	53.0	49.2	45.1	39.5	32.1
Total	39.3	36.2	32.8	30.7	23.7

Rural

	1	2	3	4	5
Male	58.9	42.5	42.5	67.2	29.4
Female	83.1	72.0	72.0	82.0	57.2
Total	71.5	57.7	57.5	74.8	40.7

1 : Chichaoua ; 2 : Taroudant ; 3 : Sous-Massa ; 4 : Figuig ; 5 : Greater Casablanca

Secondly, the degree of asymmetry in this distribution also shows notable evolution. Let us recall that the degree of asymmetry measured by the two Fisher indices gives us information on the homogeneity of distribution and therefore on the population studied. If the distribution of illiteracy were distributed normally, the value of the coefficient would be nil.

The distribution of illiteracy for men is more greatly asymmetric to the right as the value of the index moves from 0.35 to 1.4. This result means that the distribution of illiteracy among males tends to be less homogenous. For women, on the other hand, it tends toward homogenization, the value of the coefficient advancing from −1.636 to 0.169, i.e. coming close to zero.

3/ RELATIONSHIP BETWEEN ILLITERACY AND SOCIO-ECONOMIC VARIABLES

It is possible to analyse illiteracy rates according to age, marital status, professional activity and even residential type as data from the census of 2004 distinguishes between rural and urban. The aim is to explain the variation in rates of illiteracy according to the sociological and economic variables mentioned above.

In principle, schooling opportunities corresponding to public policy in education, address mainly the young. All other things being equal, the strong relationship between age and the fall in illiteracy indirectly expresses the impact of public policy. It is reasonable to assume that if the value of the correlation between age and the illiteracy rate is stronger in the Sahara than for Sous-Massa or for any other region of Morocco, one could deduce that public supply was higher in the first rather than the second. This conclusion assumes that the individuals have the same demand curve, whatever the place of residence.

For this purpose, we first deal with the analysis of the correlation matrices between the variables, before attempting to determine the most appropriate regression models.

What lessons might be drawn from the correlation matrices found in the appendices?

1/ Apart from a few exceptions, the structure of the correlations is practically the same for males regardless of their place of residence. The correlations are negative for individuals from 6 to 14 years of age and from 15 to 59 years of age, in other words, the rate of illiteracy decreases when the percentage of young people rises, but increases with that of older people. This result provides a first indication of the positive effect of the public policy of systematic schooling conducted in the Saharan provinces. The rate of activity is strongly and positively correlated with the illiteracy rate for males in both environments. This result is explainable by the fact that, in the past, older people did not receive the same schooling before entering the job market.

2/ This also applies to women due to the strong relationship of positive dependence illiteracy and people under 15 years of age or over 60. But there is a negative correlation in the dependent variable studies and the rate of individuals of 15 to 59 years of age in both rural and urban areas. To the contrary of what has just been noted about males, the rate of activity has almost no relationship with the illiteracy of females.

Let us begin by analysing illiteracy according to age, prior to proceeding to a more in-depth study taking into consideration the entire age distribution as well as other variables explaining the rate of illiteracy.

The first and most important conclusion I can deduce from these analyses, is that, as expected, there is a relationship—sometimes non linear—between age and illiteracy. Progressively, as age rises, the illiteracy rate also increases. In other words, in the Sahara like elsewhere, on average, young people show the lowest rates of illiteracy. This trend is explainable by the high supply of school places in the educational system offered by the public authorities, and rising demand on the part of families who understand the relationship been schooling and employment, or other variables connected to the modernization of society.

However, the relationship between age and illiteracy for individuals of 6 to 14 years of age does pose a problem. The result of the analysis is counter intuitive. I expected to see a negative relationship between the two variables: as this population is young, it was normal to predict a negative relationship between the percentage of the young in ecological units and the rate of illiteracy. However, nothing could be further from the truth, firstly, because the values of the linear model are not significant and are indicative of the absence of relationship between the variables studied, and secondly, because the curvilinear model is not satisfactory in so far as it cannot be interpreted even if the explained variance percentage is significant. Indeed, it is 35.7%.

Table 5.3: *Regression analysis between the rate of illiteracy and percentage of people under 6 to 14 years of age*

Dependent variable: Rate of illiteracy								
Equation	**Model Summary**					**Parameter Estimates**		
	R square	**F**	**dif1**	**dif2**	**Sig.**	**Constant**	**b1**	**b2**
Linear	.000	.006	1	113	.940	45.697	.021	
Quadratic	.211	15.016	2	112	.000	87.985	−5.867	.180

The independent variable is population under 6 to 14 years of age.

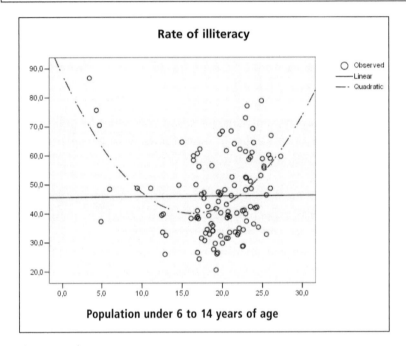

How can such an anomaly be explained? The first assumption I can make is that I probably combine heterogeneous populations in the same analysis. Let us begin by breaking down the population according to gender, a variable that is strongly correlated to illiteracy. The following tables and graphs depict the regression models for each gender.

Two different regression models for boys and girls are observed, the parameter values of which are all statistically significant. For the first, when the percentage of young men in the communes increases, illiteracy decreases. The relationship is reversed for girls. So one can

Table 5.4: *Regression analysis between rate of illiteracy and the percentage of people from 15 to 59 years of age*

	Dependent variable: Rate of illiteracy							
Equation	**Model Summary**					**Parameter Estimates**		
	R square	**F**	**dif1**	**dif2**	**Sig.**	**Constant**	**b1**	**b2**
Linear	.008	.923	1	113	.339	54.996	−.146	
Quadratic	.357	31.038	2	112	.000	363.873	−9.511	.069
The independent variable is population under 15 to 59 years of age.								

Rate of illiteracy

Population under 15 to 59 years of age

understand why, by mixing the two sub-populations, as was done in the first analysis, we do not obtain any relationship between the two variables studied.

Taking into consideration not only the age distribution but also the rate of activity and the rate of singlehood, the following regression models are obtained and the stepwise procedure constructed.

$$Y_{HR} = 39.787 - 1.497\,X_2 + 1.576\,X_5$$

$$Y_{FR} = 201.98 - 2.796\,X_2 + 2.011\,X_3 + 0.619\,X_5$$

Table 5.5: *Regression analysis between the rate of illiteracy and the percentage of population 60 years of age and older*

Equation	Dependent variable: Rate of illiteracy							
	Model Summary					Parameter Estimates		
	R square	F	dif1	dif2	Sig.	Constant	b1	b2
Linear	.117	14.966	1	113	.000	34.904	1.388	
Quadratic	.126	8.063	2	112	.001	40.569	−.179	.091
The independent variable is population 60 years of age and older.								

Population under 60 years of age and older

$$Y_{HU} = 50.822 - 1.92\, X_2 + 1.783\, X_5$$

$$Y_{FU} = 206 - 2.932\, X_2 + 2.392\, X_3 + 0.503\, X_5$$

Y, the illiteracy rate to be explained, is indexed by H: men; F: women; R: rural; U: urban. X_1 is the percentage of individuals from 6 to 14 years of age, X_2, the percentage aged between 15 and 59 years, X_3 individuals aged over 60, X_4, singles, and X_5 the rate of activity in each commune.

Table 5.6: *Regression analysis between the illiteracy rate and percentage of boys from 6 to 14 years of age*

Equation	Model Summary					Parameter Estimates		
	R square	F	dif1	dif2	Sig.	Constant	b1	b2
Linear	.102	12.875	1	113	.000	48.659	−.724	
Quadratic	.214	15.280	2	112	.000	69.822	−3.480	.077

The independent variable is population under 6 to 14 years of age.

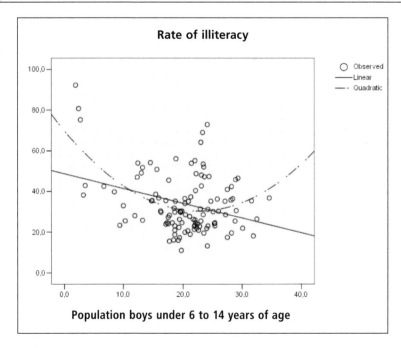

It should be pointed out that the four regression models explain the significant share of variance in illiteracy, of 37.3%, 66.1%, 39.2%, and 57.3%, respectively.

It should be noted that the structure of the regression equations for men is identical for urban and rural areas. The only differences are in the estimated values of the parameters. Moreover, apart from a difference between the values of constant β_0 for the two equations (39.787 and 50.822), that gives only the intersecting point in the plane formed by X_2 and X_5 and the axis bearing Y, even if the estimated val-

Table 5.7: *Regression analysis between the illiteracy rate and the percentage of girls 6 to 14 years of age*

Dependent variable: Rate of illiteracy								
Equation	**Model Summary**					**Parameter Estimates**		
	R square	**F**	**dif1**	**dif2**	**Sig.**	**Constant**	**b1**	**b2**
Linear	.100	12.502	1	113	.001	22.920	1.680	
Quadratic	.153	10.134	2	112	.000	149.712	−11.516	.337
The independent variable is population under 6 to 14 years of age.								

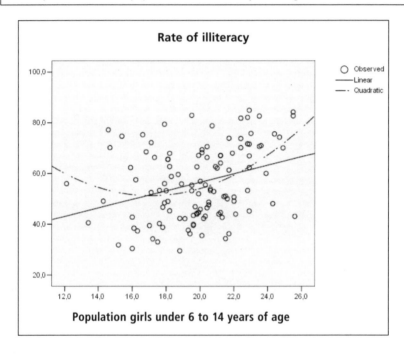

Population girls under 6 to 14 years of age

ues of parameters β_1, X_2 and X_5 for the sole variable considered as the most relevant for describing the rate of illiteracy, are practically identical and, especially of identical sign. This means that both planes are almost parallel.

The same remarks hold true for the regression equations for women in rural and urban environments.

The big difference between regression models for men and women is due to the fact that, in the first instance, variable X_3 exerts no significant influence, whereas it does for the second.

The illiteracy rate appears strongly but negatively influenced by the proportion of people between 15 and 59 years of age, for males as well as females. In other terms, when the proportion of population between 15 and 59 years of age increases, the illiteracy rate tends to decrease. As might be expected, a rise in the proportion of population of 60 and over strengthens the rate of illiteracy. This finding corresponds to what is known elsewhere about illiteracy and its variation according to generation, i.e. the young are comparatively much less illiterate than older people.

Now let us take into consideration the relationship between illiteracy and activity. The variable to be explained is positively determined by the rate of activity in rural and urban communes. However, it is less so for women than for men. In other terms, when the rate of activity increases in the communes, the rate of illiteracy also increases, but this increase is stronger for males than for females. Activity is more of an aggravating source of illiteracy for men than for women. This result can be accounted for by the lower proportion of working women.

It might be argued that older people, both male and female, not having been to school at the normal schooling age, and entering into the job market, see their rate of illiteracy reach a high level. The explanation is reinforced by the correlations between age and illiteracy, and occupational activity and illiteracy.

We will summarize all the preceding hypotheses by the theoretical causal structure linking the three variables for both genders.

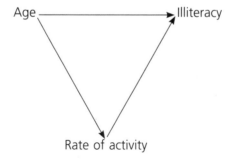

PRINCIPAL CONCLUSIONS

Regardless of the measurement used, it can be observed that over the past three decades the Saharan regions saw:

1/ A drastic drop in the rate of illiteracy falling from nearly 95% to less than 40%.

2/ This drop is much greater in these regions than in other similar provinces of Morocco. The regions of the Sahara were more advantaged than Sous Massa, the second great economic centre of the Kingdom. This essential finding is explainable more by supply than by individual demand. One can assume that if demand were the determinant factor accounting for the drop in illiteracy, Sous Massa should be better off than the Saharan regions. This, however, is not the case.

3/ The illiteracy distributions according to gender are unequal from one region and one residential area to the next.

4/ However, it is noteworthy that the fall in illiteracy is higher for females than for males. It could even be said such sex-based inequality will no longer be in effect by 2020.

The Saharan regions have clearly benefited from very effective positive discrimination that can be explained by the determination of the Moroccan Government to compensate for the conditions of deprivation the Sahrawis went through during the times of Spanish colonization. The supply by the state in terms of education is visible when considering the number of places offered to the users of the educational system in the Saharan provinces, as is shown in the following chapter.

APPENDIX TO CHAPTER 5

Table 5.8: *Evolution of illiteracy in the Sahara*

		1982		1994		2004	
		Male	Female	Male	Female	Male	Female
N	Valid	8	8	90	90	115	115
	Lack	0	0	0	0	0	0
Mean		54.9350	83.6350	45.2402	73.4713	33.978	56.356
Median		56.3750	83.2050	42.8150	78.0050	30.300	53.900
Mode		39.89(a)	74.40(a)	34.87	.00	24.5(a)	44.0(a)
Standard deviation		10.02474	8.94813	16.14040	20.20022	14.5573	14.4367
Variance		100.495	80.069	260.513	408.049	211.915	208.419
Skewness		.339	.409	.350	−1.636	1.401	.169
Skewness standard deviation		.752	.752	.254	.254	.226	.226
Kurtosis		.847	−1.485	−.717	3.808	2.498	−1.018
Kurtosis standard deviation		1.481	1.481	.503	.503	.447	.447

Table 5.9: *Correlations between illiteracy and independent variables (2004)*

Men (rural areas)

		Population under 6 to 14 years	Population under 15 to 59 years	Population aged 60 and over	Singles	Illiteracy rate	Activity rate
Population under 6 to 14 years	Pearson Correlation	1	-.945(**)	.479(**)	-.728(**)	-.335(**)	-.929(**)
	Sig.		.000	.000	.000	.004	.000
	N	74	74	74	74	74	74
Population under 15 to 59 years	Pearson Correlation	-.945(**)	1	-.694(**)	.794(**)	.289(*)	.943(**)
	Sig.	.000		.000	.000	.012	.000
	N	74	74	74	74	74	74
Population aged 60 and over	Pearson Correlation	.479(**)	-.694(**)	1	-.580(**)	-.105	-.596(**)
	Sig.	.000	.000		.000	.374	.000
	N	74	74	74	74	74	74
Single	Pearson Correlation	-.728(**)	.794(**)	-.580(**)	1	.169	.733(**)
	Sig.	.000	.000	.000		.150	.000
	N	74	74	74	74	74	74
Illiteracy rate	Pearson Correlation	-.335(**)	.289(*)	-.105	.169	1	.451(**)
	Sig.	.004	.012	.374	.150		.000
	N	74	74	74	74	74	74
Activity rate	Pearson Correlation	-.929(**)	.943(**)	-.596(**)	.733(**)	.451(**)	1
	Sig.	.000	.000	.000	.000	.000	
	N	74	74	74	74	74	74

** Correlation is significant at the 0.01 level (2-tailed). * Correlation is significant at the 0.05 level (2-tailed).

Women (rural areas)

		Population under 6 to 14 years	Population under 15 to 59 years	Population aged 60 and over	Singles	Illiteracy rate	Activity rate
Population under 6 to 14 years	Pearson Correlation	1	-.772(**)	-.279(*)	-.097	-.412(**)	-.257(*)
	Sig.		.000	.016	.412	.000	.027
	N	74	74	74	74	74	74
Population under 15 to 59 years	Pearson Correlation	-.772(**)	1	-.192	.384(**)	-.638(**)	.442(**)
	Sig.	.000		.101	.001	.000	.000
	N	74	74	74	74	74	74
Population aged 60 and over	Pearson Correlation	-.279(*)	-.192	1	-.023	.455(**)	-.224
	Sig.	.016	.101		.847	.000	.055
	N	74	74	74	74	74	74
Single	Pearson Correlation	-.097	.384(**)	-.023	1	.050	.396(**)
	Sig.	.412	.001	.847		.672	.000
	N	74	74	74	74	74	74
Illiteracy rate	Pearson Correlation	-.412(**)	-.638(**)	.455(**)	.050	1	.001
	Sig.	.000	.000	.000	.672		.996
	N	74	74	74	74	74	74
Activity rate	Pearson Correlation	-.257(*)	.442(**)	-.224	.396(**)	.001	1
	Sig.	.027	.000	.055	.000	.996	
	N	74	74	74	74	74	74

** Correlation is significant at the 0.01 level (2-tailed). * Correlation is significant at the 0.05 level (2-tailed).

Table 5.9: Continued

Men (urban areas)

		Population under 6 to 14 years	Population under 15 to 59 years	Population aged 60 and over	Singles	Illiteracy rate	Activity rate
Population under 6 to 14 years	Pearson Correlation	1	-.989(**)	.598(**)	-.606(**)	-.429(**)	-.982(**)
	Sig.		.000	.000	.000	.005	.000
	N	41	41	41	41	41	41
Population under 15 to 59 years	Pearson Correlation	-.989(**)	1	-.659(**)	.601(**)	.405(**)	.971(**)
	Sig.	.000		.000	.000	.009	.000
	N	41	41	41	41	41	41
Population aged 60 and over	Pearson Correlation	.598(**)	-.659(**)	1	-.055	-.139	-.600(**)
	Sig.	.000	.000		.732	.387	.000
	N	41	41	41	41	41	41
Single	Pearson Correlation	-.606(**)	.601(**)	-.055	1	.420(**)	.626(**)
	Sig.	.000	.000	.732		.006	.000
	N	41	41	41	41	41	41
Illiteracy rate	Pearson Correlation	-.429(**)	.405(**)	-.139	.420(**)	1	.507(**)
	Sig.	.005	.009	.387	.006		.001
	N	41	41	41	41	41	41
Activity rate	Pearson Correlation	-.982(**)	.971(**)	-.600(**)	.626(**)	.507(**)	1
	Sig.	.000	.000	.000	.000	.001	
	N	41	41	41	41	41	41

** Correlation is significant at the 0.01 level (2-tailed).

Women (urban areas)

		Population under 6 to 14 years	Population under 15 to 59 years	Population aged 60 and over	Singles	Illiteracy rate	Activity rate
Population under 6 to 14 years	Pearson Correlation	1	-.860(**)	-.185	-.187	.331(*)	-.641(**)
	Sig.		.000	.247	.242	.035	.000
	N	41	41	41	41	41	41
Population under 15 to 59 years	Pearson Correlation	-.860(**)	1	-.032	.242	-.494(**)	.687(**)
	Sig.	.000		.842	.128	.001	.000
	N	41	41	41	41	41	41
Population aged 60 and over	Pearson Correlation	-.185	-.032	1	.725(**)	.543(**)	.016
	Sig.	.247	.842		.000	.000	.921
	N	41	41	41	41	41	41
Single	Pearson Correlation	-.187	.242	.725(**)	1	.350(*)	.250
	Sig.	.242	.128	.000		.025	.115
	N	41	41	41	41	41	41
Illiteracy rate	Pearson Correlation	.331(*)	-.494(**)	.543(**)	.350(*)	1	-.154
	Sig.	.035	.001	.000	.025		.337
	N	41	41	41	41	41	41
Activity rate	Pearson Correlation	-.641(**)	.687(**)	.016	.250	-.154	1
	Sig.	.000	.000	.921	.115	.337	
	N	41	41	41	41	41	41

** Correlation is significant at the 0.01 level (2-tailed). * Correlation is significant at the 0.05 level (2-tailed).

6

Substantial and Rapid Increase in School Enrolment in the Sahara

From Case Study to Generalization

It is not particularly easy to assess a public policy, to gauge its influence and to know if it has reached its objectives. Although it may seem simple, this exercise gives rise to considerable theoretical and methodological problems. The reader will forgive me for indulging in the details of the demonstration. That will however be the cost to pay to check if the objective set in this chapter has been achieved.

Firstly, the two phenomena we are about to study, namely public policy and school enrolment, are located at two levels of reality. The first is an essentially social phenomenon while the second is intrinsically individual as it is simply an aggregation of individual behaviours. Then, two levels of reality, the macro-sociological and micro-sociological, are combined.[1] Their analyses raise the problem of moving from one level of reality to another, which is not easy to accomplish. The solution sociologists agree upon, when they take the issue seriously, consists of constructing a transition mechanism from one level to the next.

Furthermore, identifying and measuring the influence of public policy on school enrolment has to be conducted in two phases. In the first phase, it is necessary to test the assumption according to which supply precedes demand for school enrolment. In the second phase, one would have to analyse in detail public supply, schooling demand

and real or achieved schooling, these last two variables are not necessarily identical. In fact, school demand by the users of the educational system can be far above or below the real number of enrolled pupils. Besides, as the three variables do change overtime, we should study their evolution models as well as the parameter values of these models: the objective being to know whether the intensity of growth rates of supply is above the actual level of schooling. If the two assumptions prove to be confirmed, we can then conclude that the influence of the educational policy on actual schooling is more significant than demand as formulated by families regardless of public supply.[2]

Without having any detailed data for all the regions of the Sahara, I had to rely on the understanding and competency of the officer in charge of the regional administrative service of the Ministry of National Education, to gather regional statistics on school enrolment in Laayoune-Boujdour-Sakia-El-Hamra from 1976 to 2007. They are of great interest and enable me, not only to describe the models of change in school enrolment, but also to identify the type of relationship between the evolution of the frequencies of the enrolled students and the number of places available in elementary and secondary school institutions, an excellent indicator of public policy. I endeavour to generalize the results of these analyses by using the less detailed data on school enrolment in the Sahara since 1980–81.

1/ EVOLUTION OF SCHOOL ENROLMENT

Let us begin by analysing the growth in school enrolment from 1976 to 2007.

In each phase in the analysis of these longitudinal data, I provide a graph corresponding to each statistical series, the most appropriate mathematical model(s) to describe them, and an attempt at interpretation.

Let us begin with primary education. Figure 6.1 simply reproduces the total number of pupils all sexes combined on the one hand, and the number of female children enrolled on the other hand. A quick glance reveals that the two curves are similar, develop at the same rate, and perhaps follow the same model. They also indicate that after a period of rapid expansion, we apparently come close to a saturation threshold.

The plot of this longitudinal variable and the brief analysis of the differences between their coordinates seem to indicate the existence of a geometrical progression. If we add to these observations the data

Table 6.1: *School enrolment data for Laayoune, Boujdour, Sakya El Hamra*

	Number of pupils (elementary)	Number of girls (elementary)	Number of pupils (secondary)	Number of girls (secondary)	Number of pupils second cycle (secondary)	Number of girls in second cycle (secondary)
1976–77	3,061	485	0	0	0	0
1980–81	7,712	2,939	841	177	82	17
1989–90	12,262	5,446	6,374	2,741	1,434	515
1999–00	31,749	14,574	11,187	5,700	5,089	2,190
2006–07	32,273	15,350	16,364	8,009	8,704	4,572

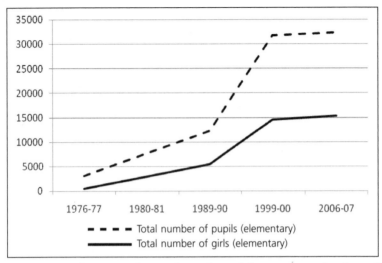

Figure 6.1: *Evolution in the total number of elementary school pupils (total number & girls)*

from the earlier Spanish census, it would be noted that at the outset, the evolution of the total number of pupils enrolled in primary education is slow indeed. Very quickly, progress in school enrolment went through a cumulative process starting exactly in 1975. This will be obvious upon analysing the data for all the Sahara since 1964, as presented in the third section of this chapter. Naturally, the process is not infinite as it is dependent not only on investment, but especially, on the limited size of potential school enrolment in primary education. The differential equation describing the assumption of unlimited growth is:

$$dx/ dt = \beta x \qquad\qquad [1]$$

where β is the growth parameter assumed to be constant. For 0 and x = 1 and by integrating the equation [1], an exponential model is obtained that we transform into an intrinsically linear model to estimate the parameters according to the least square method. This gives:

$$\ln x = \ln \alpha + \beta\, t \qquad\qquad [2]$$

which actually is a straight line equation. The parameters of the model to be estimated are α and β. The estimated values of β and α are 0.613 and 1978.23, respectively. The fit is almost perfect, with the value of R^2

being equal to 94%. That means that the model "explains" 94% of the variance observed.

Irrespective of technical considerations and despite the degree of fit that it allows, this model is only partially satisfactory in so far as it does not take into consideration the existence of the saturation threshold. On the one hand, the total number of pupils ready to enter primary education is not infinite, which the exponential model assumes. On the other hand, the real data indicate that we have reached the saturation threshold or, at least, we are approaching it. Here, it is to be noted that the rate of net school enrolment in primary education is currently approximately equal to 100%. The logistic model is the one that describes more realistically the cumulative process already mentioned above, as well as the existence of the saturation threshold.

Let us recall the assumptions entailed in the construction of this mathematical model. Let us call α the level of saturation. This is the maximum size of the potential school enrolment population in primary education. The x is the number of enrolments in time t; $(\alpha - x)$ will be equal to the distance separating x from α. The rate of growth of x per time unit is proportional to x and $(\alpha - x)$. Formally, this results in the following equation:

$$dx/dt = kx (\alpha - x) \tag{3}$$

where k designates the coefficient of proportionality. As can be seen, x, which grows over time, is an acceleration factor. On the other hand, $(\alpha - x)$ is a retarding factor. While the size of the first increases over time, that of the second decreases. Gradually, as one approaches saturation threshold α, the magnitude $(\alpha - x)$ tends toward zero, as the rate of growth dx/dt also does.

The logistical function has the following form:

$$x = \alpha / [1 + \beta \exp (-Yt)] \tag{4}$$

This kind of function is sometimes called "general law of economic development". It fits the type of diffusion over time of a great number of social and economic phenomena. Let us recall that the French sociologist Gabriel Tarde (1890) was the first one to identify and later apply it to diffusion phenomena.[3]

Estimation of the parameters of the logistic function does not pose any technical problem as we know the saturation threshold which is

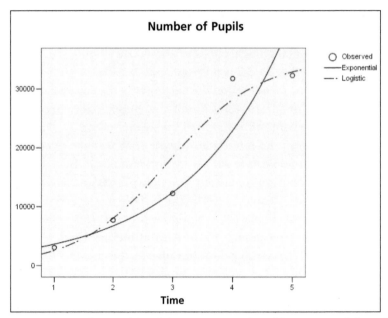

Figure 6.2: *Goodness of fit of the exponential and logistic models with the evolution of the total number of enrolments in primary education*

the ordinate of the maximum asymptote of the function. This threshold of course may fluctuate over the forthcoming years, but it will most likely remain near this value. The following graph represents the points observed and the two models estimated. The value R^2 for the logistic model is equal to 93%. It is slightly under that given by the exponential model.

In conclusion, the two models fit perfectly with the data, the logistic model being more realistic in so far as it integrates the fundamental data relative to the saturation threshold.

We end up with the same conclusions for the situation of enrolments of girls in elementary schools. The only significant difference deserving note is that the logistic model fits slightly better with the data, than the exponential model: R^2 is equal to 97% for the first and 95% for the second.

One cannot reasonably expect to find similar types of evolution for the elementary and secondary education cycles, the latter being designated as "qualifying". For both of these populations, the evolution is in a period of strong expansion that will most likely accelerate, only reaching the saturation threshold at a later date. In 1975, we started

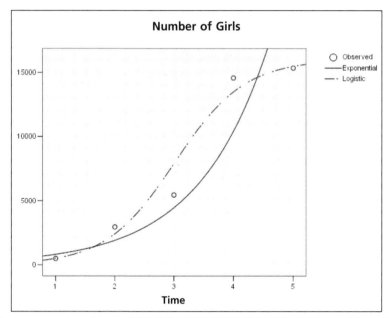

Figure 6.3: *Goodness of fit of the exponential and logistic models with the evolution of the total number of girls enrolled in primary education*

from scratch. At that date, when Morocco recovered its Saharan provinces, not even a single secondary educational institution existed.

The following graphs represent the situation of the growing number of enrolments in secondary education. Even though the net rates of school enrolment are equal to 82.53% for pupils between 12 and 14 years of age enrolled in the first cycle, and 68.75% for those enrolled in the second cycle, we are still far from reaching the saturation threshold. It is true that we can predict this threshold and the year in which it will be reached, but for the time being, it is more prudent to limit oneself to reality.

These situations show practically constant growth levels. They all follow a linear model. The value of R^2 equals 97% for the linear model and 70% for the exponential model. This is confirmed by the statistical fit of the data. To keep the study simple, I present only the linear and exponential goodness of fit of the number of enrolments in the first secondary cycle. There is an identical goodness of fit for the other models.

It goes without saying that these models are indicative of the past and present only—and certainly not the future. Indeed, we know that

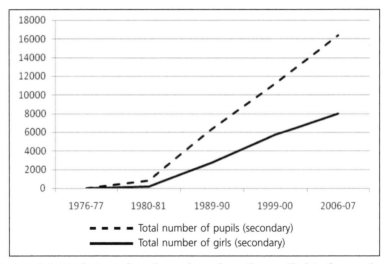

Figure 6.4: *Evolution of total number of pupils enrolled in first cycle secondary education (total number and girls)*

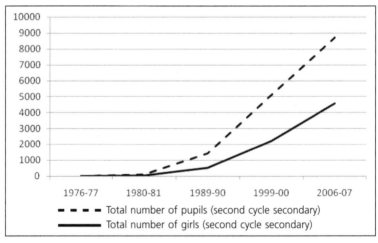

Figure 6.5: *Evolution of the number of enrolments in second cycle secondary education (total number and girls)*

there will be a changing situation in the total number of enrolments in first cycle elementary and second cycle secondary education, and progressively as we approach the saturation threshold, acceleration of the curve will necessarily change and take on the form of a logistic function.

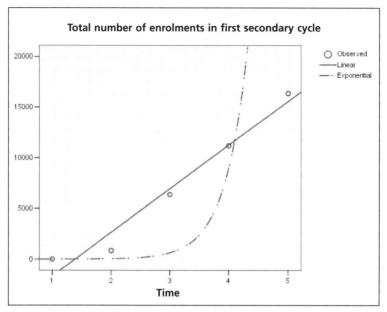

Figure 6.6: *Fitting of linear and exponential models with the situation in the number of enrolments in the first secondary cycle*

One conclusion is clear: the evolution of school enrolment in this vast Saharan region largely support the initial assumption according to which young Sahrawis have not only bridged the huge gap separating them from other Moroccans, but they have actually done even better.

Currently, their net rates of school enrolment for all ages greatly exceed the national rate and even those of all the other regions of Morocco, except Casablanca and Rabat. However, they come close to it. Better still, the rates of net school enrolment in Oued Ed-Dahab for 6 and 15–17 year olds are greater than those for Casablanca and Rabat. The data shown in the following table leaves no shadow of doubt on this issue.

2/ TESTING THE HYPOTHESES OF THE INFLUENCE OF EDUCATIONAL POLICY

The explanation of the evolution in school enrolment in the Sahara, like everywhere else, gives rise to problems that are always tricky to solve in an entirely satisfactory manner. In fact, I do not have complete data from the sociological surveys conducted on this question. We know

Table 6.2: *Specific rates of school enrolment (2004–2005)*

Regions	6 years of age	6–11 years of age	12–14 years of age	15–17 years of age
Oued Ed-Dahab – Lagouira	99.35%	99.17%	84.38%	77.88%
Laayoune – Boujdour – Sakia El Hamra	92.08%	95.75%	82.53%	68.75%
Guelmim – Es-Smara	83.39%	87.94%	81.54%	63.82%
Sous-Massa – Draa	90.59%	92.44%	74.31%	44.36%
Gharb – Chrarda – Beni Hssen	97.18%	88.96%	61.37%	34.88%
Chaouia – Ourdigha	86.86%	90.54%	63.97%	37.44%
Marrakech – Tensift – Al Haouz	86.98%	90.85%	64.04%	32.86%
L'Oriental	83.66%	93.36%	68.96%	40.49%
Grand Casablanca	96.43%	102.84%	95.93%	70.27%
Rabat – Salé – Zemmour – Zaer	95.99%	101.48%	93.55%	67.99%
Doukkala – Abda	86.38%	88.85%	55.95%	32.81%
Tadla – Azilal	89.82%	91.57%	63.01%	37.93%
Meknès – Tafilalet	91.80%	95.35%	80.30%	51.83%
Fès – Boulmane	89.36%	96.70%	76.36%	53.37%
Taza – Al Hoceima – Taounate	82.61%	81.64%	50.75%	27.10%
Tanger – Tétouan	85.59%	90.61%	61.43%	35.61%
National	89.58%	92.85%	70.62%	44.28%

Note: The gross rates of school enrolment are a measure of the number of children available for enrolment against the number actually in school. Thus the apparently anomalous statistic that shows that in 2004 more than 100% of the age group 6/11 were enrolled is inflated because the number of children in primary education included some who are aged more than 11.

that school enrolment is the result of individual supply and demand for places in the educational system. Supply is unquestionably the best indicator for measuring public policy. Other indicators also exist such as the age of mandatory school attendance.

In this section, I propose to test the relationship between the number of elementary and secondary schools, and the total number of enrolments. Although the evolution in the number of schools is strongly linked to the total number of pupils enrolled, if it is the case that the first precedes the second in time, one could conclude that these is a strong influence of public policy on school enrolment.

To do this, I shall proceed in two steps. The first step consists of studying the growth model in the number of schools. The second step will entail the study of the relationships between variables via appropriate regression models.

Firstly, we note that the value of the slope of the linear regression model representing growth in the number of primary schools is slightly higher than that of the model representing growth in the number of

Table 6.3: *Evolution in the number of schools*

	Number of elementary school institutions	Number of first cycle schools	Number of secondary cycle schools
1976–77	6	0	0
1980–81	14	2	1
1989–90	22	7	2
1999–00	39	14	6
2006–07	47	14	8

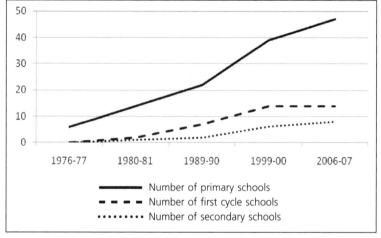

Figure 6.7: *Growth in number of schools*

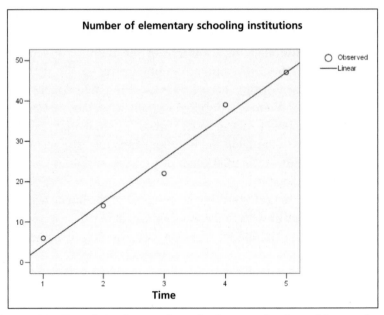

Figure 6.8: *Growth in the number of primary schools and its goodness of fit with the regression model*

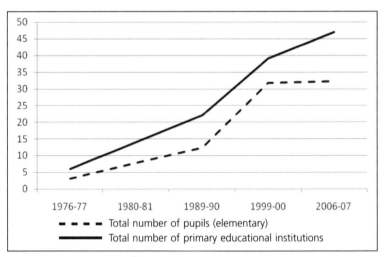

Figure 6.9: *Comparison of growth in the number of primary schools and the total number of enrolments.*

school enrolments in the elementary schooling system. The first one is equal to 0.99, and the second to 0.95. So that the reader can easily apprehend this capital point without necessarily having to refer to

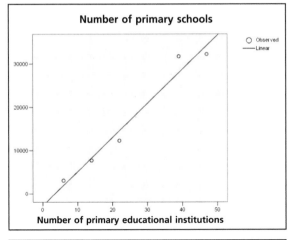

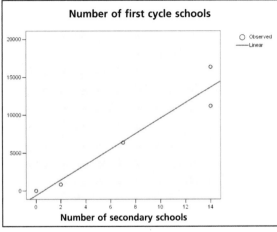

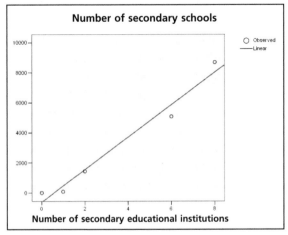

Figure 6.10: *Relationship between the number of schools and the total number of enrolments*

model-building, I suggest a graphic comparison in the growth in the number of elementary schooling institutions and the total number of enrolments therein. The scales have been modified so the comparison between the two rates of growth will be visible.

The conclusion to draw from the first step of this demonstration is that the supply of places in the educational system not only preceded demand but that its growth rate was steadier than the growth rate in demand itself.

Secondly, the regression models showing the relationships between the number of schools and the total number of enrolments in the different institutions are also very eloquent. Whether for elementary or second cycle education, the result is identical, i.e. progressively as the number of schools rises, the total number of pupils enrolled in such institutions increases in the same proportion.

It is noteworthy that the goodness of fit is almost perfect. The percentage of explained variance amounts to 97%. No other model gives any additional information or precise data on the relationship between supply and demand in school enrolment.

Conclusion

Because of the non-availability of data that would have enabled the to measure the demand in school enrolment and compare it to supply, I can, however, take as a reasonable foundation the results of previous analyses, to formulate the following propositions.

1/ I suggest that the supply in seats in the educational system is a good indicator of the policy adopted by the public authorities.
2/ From 1975 to 2007, the growth rates in supply are slightly higher than those of school enrolment.
3/ Supply precedes growth in school enrolment.
4/ The relationships between supply and school enrolment are exceptionally strong and perfectly described by a linear model.

Based on these four proposals established empirically, I may conclude that the schooling policy applied has had a decisive impact on the growth in elementary and secondary schooling in the Sahara region.

3/ GENERALIZATION OF THESE RESULTS TO THE SAHARAN PROVINCES

Am I in a position to generalize these conclusions to all regions of the Sahara? There are statistics for all the Sahara. They are, however, less

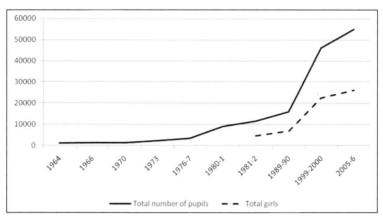

Figure 6.11: *Growth of enrolled pupils in the primary school for all the Sahara (Overall and girls)*

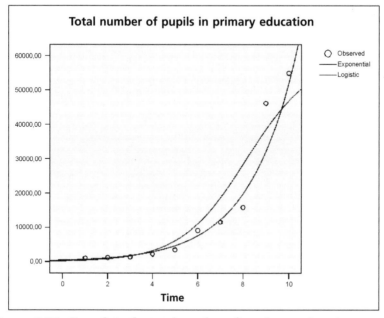

Figure 6.12: *Growth in the total number of enrolments in primary education schools and its modelling (1964–2006)*

significant than those gathered for the region of Laayoune-Boujdour. They deal with four points of observation corresponding to the years 1981–82, 1989–90, 1999–2000, and 2005–06. There is only one series

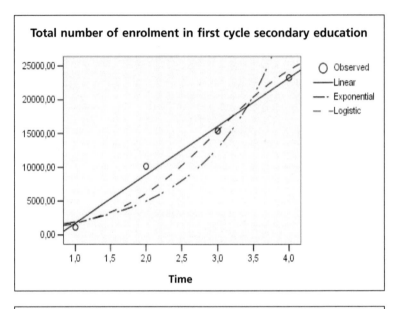

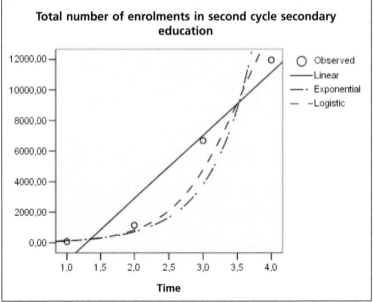

Figure 6.13: *Growth in the number of enrolments in the first and second cycles of secondary education and their modelling*

of complete statistics concerning primary education collated from Spanish and Moroccan sources since 1964.

The growth in the total number of pupils for primary education can be described by an exponential model or a logistic curve as shown in Figure 6.12. The exponential model better describes the real data than the logistic curve, even though both are statistically significant. It can be seen that the first one explains a higher percentage of variance (96.6%) than the second (89.8%).

The reader should not expect such precise information for other areas of growth as it concerns only four observation points. Generally, the results of the study concerning the Laayoune-Boujdour region can be readily generalized to the entire Sahara. By way of illustration and comparison, we will present the results of the goodness of fit statistics for the total number of pupils enrolled in the first and second cycles of secondary education.

What can one deduce from a systematic analysis of all provinces of the Sahara, about the relationship between the total number of pupils enrolled at the different levels of elementary and secondary education and the independent variables constituted by the total number of pupils enrolled in schools, the number of classes and the number of teachers? All the variables are closely linked. These results corroborate those we previously established for the region of Laayoune-Boujdour alone. The values of the parameters of the straight lines in the regression tables describing these relationships are all significant. Generally, they explain a percentage in variance, depending on the case, varying from 90 to 99%.

CONCLUSION

We can generalize the conclusions deduced from analysis of the data for the Laayoune-Boujdour region to the entire Sahara, namely that public supply precedes and strongly determines educational demand.

It is easy to show that the net rates of school enrolment in the Sahara are by far superior to those in all other regions of Morocco. For lack of complete longitudinal data for the regions of the Sahara from 1975 to the present, I will limit myself to showing, through the graphs appended to this chapter the evolution of these rates for Morocco and a few observation points regarding the Sahara.

NOTES

1. An intrinsically social phenomenon is one that cannot be reduced to the sum of individual behaviours. A social but intrinsically individual phenomenon results from the aggregation of individual behaviours. School enrolment is an illustration of this second type of phenomena. The same applies to several social phenomena such as the outcome of election ballots or the consumption of goods. A social policy, a legislation, any act undertaken by a corporate actor like the government are intrinsically social phenomena. Other instances include norms, the structure of a market or a political organization. These phenomena can be reduced to their components. The same problem is encountered in natural sciences, such as physics or biology. The reader can refer to the systematic study that I made of this issue in Cherkaoui (2005).

2. This problem is partially dealt with by Boudon (1973, 1979, 1998), Coleman (1990) and by myself in Cherkaoui (2005, 2006) and Hedström (2005). If one distinguishes the political decision from time t_1 (DPt_1), the effects on individuals (EI), individual actions (AI) and school enrolment at the global level in relation to time t_2 (St_2), this leads to a graph representing all the relationships between the macro-sociological variables (top of graph) and the micro-sociological variables (bottom of graph). This type of graph is taken from Coleman.

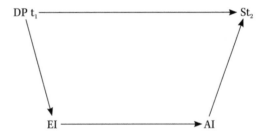

3. For a few examples of application of the logistic function to sociological phenomena, see Coleman, Katz, Mentzel (1957), and Coleman (1968). The best-known economic study is by Griliches (1957). I applied the logistic model to French data concerning the total number of baccalaureate candidates, in Cherkaoui (1982).

APPENDIX TO CHAPTER 6

The evolution of the school enrolment rates of the young aged between 6 to 11 according to sex and area of residence correspond to logistic curves. They show that we are getting to the school enrolment threshold. This threshold actually varies according to sex and residential area.

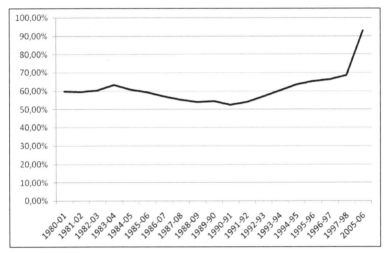

Figure 6.14: *Evolution of the net school enrolment rates of the young aged between 6 to 11 (1980–2006)*

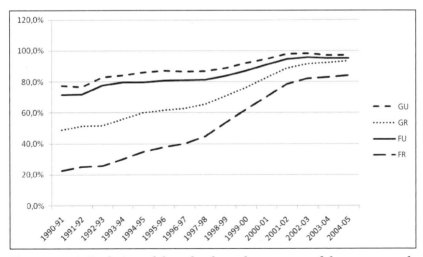

Figure 6.15: *Evolution of the school enrolment rates of the young aged between 6 to 11 by residential area and sex*

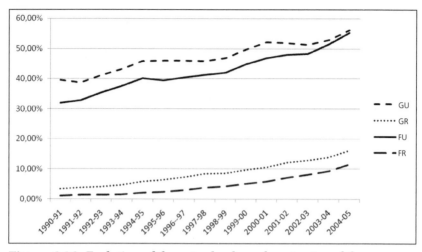

Figure 6.16: *Evolution of the net school enrolment rates of the young aged between 12 to 14 according to residential area and sex*

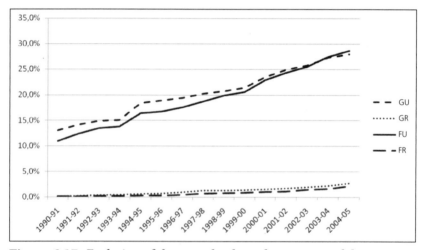

Figure 6.17: *Evolution of the net school enrolment rates of the young aged between 15 to 17 according to residential area and sex*

Key: G = Boy; F = Girl; U = Urban; R = Rural.

Let us examine the evolution of the rates of the boys living in the urban area and the girls from the rural areas, which are the extreme points. They have the same mathematical shape, but not the same saturation threshold value. In other terms, whatever the policy incentive is deployed by the public authorities to increase girls' schooling rate in the rural areas, their school rate might not reach 100%. The explanation is straightforward: it does not need further development here. It will be noticed that the inequality between these two sub-populations, which is by far the most significant, tends to shrink dramatically. In 1990–1, the gap between school enrolment of the two sub-populations was around 55%; it is now just about 13% in 2004–5.

The case is different as to school enrolment rates of the young aged between 12 to 14 and those aged between 15 and 17. For the first, inequality goes through a very worrying form of stability. Despite some progress in school enrolment at this age, inequality between urban boys and rural girls is steady in time. Contrary to what some assert, gender inequality is not significant. On the other hand, inequality according to the milieu of residence is the real handicap.

The evolution of school enrolment rates of the young aged 15 to 17 are more worrying. Inequality between the two compared sub-populations goes deeper over time. It can be seen in the evolution curves of their rates which are not parallel as they are for the young aged between 12 to 14.

Because we do not have complete data series relating to the Sahara, I have reproduced here the gross rates for these regions as compared to the national rates. It is clear then that the Sahara regions are far ahead compared to the national average.

Table 6.4: *Evolution of the gross rates of school enrolment, in the Sahara provinces, according to education level between 1994 and 2004 (in %)*

Age bracket	1994		2004	
	Saharan Provinces	Morocco	Saharan Provinces	Morocco
6/11 years	90.8	73.2	115.4	113.1
12/14 years	65.1	45.1	91.7	60.3
15/17 years	29.6	21.6	47.5	31.2
6/17 years	71.2	53.9	95.6	78.0

Note: The gross rates of school enrolment are a measure of the number of children available for enrolment against the number actually in school. Thus the apparently anomalous statistic that shows that in 2004 more than 100% of the age group 6/11 were enrolled is inflated because the number of children in primary education included some who are aged more than 11.

Source: Rates calculated based on the data from the census directories (*Annuaires statistiques*) HCP.

7

Human and Social Development

Are the hypotheses tested previously for school enrolment valid for human and social development? Have poverty and this type of development seen similar evolution in the Sahara, as with the case of literacy? Are we in a position to describe such evolution and explain it by individual variables, or on the contrary, should we consider them via factors connected to public policies? These are the issues dealt with in this chapter.

Providing an answer calls for reference to the census data as well as that from surveys on consumption and household expenditure. The High Commission for Planning has conducted extensive research according to international standards on poverty and human development. It is reliable with regard to method and data collection. Moreover, the definition of the concepts used is unequivocal and does not call for significant changes that would render any comparison invalid.

Let us begin by examining the most recent study to date in which the data from the 2004 census are analysed, along with the survey on household consumption and expenditures conducted in 2000–2001.

1/ POVERTY INDEX OF THE SAHARAN REGIONS

To enable the reader to follow future developments, it is necessary to recall the definitions of the concepts used.

The poverty rate represents the percentage of individuals for whom the standard of living is below the relative poverty line. This threshold is 1,687 DH per month for a household in urban areas composed of 5.6 members and 1,745 DH for households in rural areas composed of 6.4 members.

The poverty severity index measures the average gap between the poverty threshold and the living standards of the poorer households.

The rate of vulnerability gives the proportion of the population living under the threat of poverty. The threshold is between 1,687 and 2,531 DH per month for an urban household and 1,745 and 2,618 DH for a rural household.

The human development index takes into account health measured per life expectancy from birth, the level of education measured by the rate of literacy, and gross rate of schooling and real GNP per capita.

The social development index is the result of three indicators consisting of access to drinking water, electricity and roads.

The tables below are taken from a study conducted by the High Commission for Planning indicate the rates of poverty per region and residential area and measurement of the five indices previously defined.

Let us take a quick look at table 7.1 below.

Compared to the national average, the poverty rates of the Saharan regions—the first three in the table—are relatively lower. Only Guelmim–Es-Smara registers a poverty rate in urban areas just slightly above the national average. Overall, if residential areas are not differentiated, it can be seen that the Saharan regions register the lowest rate: only Greater Casablanca and Rabat-Salé do better. It is true that the Tangier–Tétouan region reports a rate one point lower than Guelmim–Es-Smara.

Oued Ed-Dahab–Lagouira even manages to register the lowest rate for the entire Kingdom, far ahead of the largest and most prosperous economic regions like Greater Casablanca and Rabat-Salé. The Sahrawis in this region register 1.25 times less probability of poverty than the residents of the large economic metropolis, and 5 times less than the national average. The odds ratio is quite simply equal, compared to the index values of the two regions.

Now let us take a more in-depth look at indicators of poverty, vulnerability and human and social development by province.

Let us recall that the Saharan provinces are Assa-Zag, Laayoune, Boujdour, Es-Smara, Aousserd, Oued Ed-Dahab. These provinces are shown in italics towards the end of table 7.2.

Table 7.1: *Poverty rate by region and residential area in 2004*

Region	Urban	Rural	All
Oued Ed-Dahab – Lagouira	2.9	2.3	2.8
Laayoune – Boujdour	6.2	10.1	6.3
Guelmim – Es-Smara	9.2	20.3	13.1
Sous-Massa – Draa	7.5	26.8	18.9
Gharb-chrarda – Bni Hssen	12.2	26.4	20.5
Chaouia – Ouardigha	9.4	16.7	13.5
Marrakech – Tensift – El Haouz	8.3	26.1	19.2
Oriental	13.8	24.8	17.9
Grand Casablanca	3.3	5.6	3.5
Rabat – Salé – Zemmour – Zaer	6.0	16.7	8.1
Doukala – Abda	8.7	19.5	15.6
Tadla – Azilal	9.7	17.0	14.4
Meknes – Tafilelet	10.5	31.1	19.5
Fès – Boulemane	11.0	22.8	14.2
Taza – El Hoceima – Taounate	6.9	16.9	14.5
Tangier – Tétouan	8.6	17.6	12.4
TOTAL	7.9	22.0	14.2

The first general conclusion to be drawn from a rapid examination of the index values is obvious: The Saharan regions record the lowest rates of poverty and vulnerability in the Kingdom, except for the two most developed regions of Morocco, i.e. Casablanca and Rabat. Mohammedia, a highly industrialized and agriculturally rich region, is located between Es-Samara and Aousserd. Aousserd and Oued Ed-Dahab show the lowest rate of vulnerability in the Kingdom, even lower than those of Casablanca and Rabat.

If, as was done for education, we compare the Saharan regions to other sociologically similar areas, it can be seen that the rates of poverty and vulnerability of the first are lower by twofold compared to the second. The ratios of the rates sometimes reach more than 5 in the case of Chichaoua, Figuig, and Taroudant. (This value is the result of a calculation based on the mean poverty rate (4.99) for the six Saharan

Table 7.2: *Provincial indictors of poverty, vulnerability, and human and social development*

Province	Rate (%) of		Poverty severity index in %	Provincial development indices	
	Poverty	Vulnerability		Human	Social
Zagora	33.58	25.01	4.76	0.360	0.664
Essaouira	29.80	23.79	4.40	0.342	0.220
Errachidia	29.49	20.58	5.03	0.476	0.665
Jerada	29.28	22.97	4.09	0.431	0.428
Chichaoua	29.09	27.71	3.67	0.231	0.266
Taourirt	27.29	22.84	3.52	0.485	0.368
Figuig	27.09	20.41	4.08	0.294	0.318
Tata	24.54	21.68	3.44	0.426	0.622
Azilal	23.98	25.40	2.26	0.202	0.358
Boulemane	23.85	21.14	3.15	0.326	0.470
El Kelaâ des Sraghna	23.15	28.81	2.41	0.383	0.527
Ouarzazate	22.79	21.13	3.07	0.371	0.585
Taroudant	22.59	21.08	3.00	0.408	0.471
Moulay Yacoub	22.41	22.07	2.71	0.357	0.580
El Hajeb	21.43	22.68	2.61	0.535	0.519
Sidi Kacem	21.39	24.15	2.52	0.415	0.523
Al Haouz	20.75	25.70	2.36	0.195	0.406
Tiznit	20.13	18.85	2.66	0.506	0.488
Kénitra	19.90	22.17	2.35	0.525	0.561
Khénifra	18.18	20.80	2.24	0.453	0.314
Fahs-Anjra	17.59	20.67	2.34	0.432	0.507
Nador	17.30	20.08	1.89	0.504	0.396
Chtouka Ait Baha	17.06	19.68	2.10	0.402	0.672
Sefrou	16.27	18.41	1.92	0.499	0.556
Safi	16.12	22.74	1.37	0.501	0.307
Ifrane	16.03	18.31	2.01	0.450	0.473
Chefchaouen	16.02	19.45	2.09	0.336	0.277
Khemisset	15.64	19.52	1.76	0.432	0.365
Taza	15.50	16.27	2.16	0.479	0.328
El Jadida	15.21	23.83	1.19	0.472	0.429
Taounate	14.41	16.80	1.95	0.434	0.331

Table 7.2: *Continued*

Province	Rate (%) of		Poverty severity index in %	Provincial development indices	
	Poverty	Vulnerability		Human	Social
Berkane	14.17	18.80	1.42	0.527	0.662
Benslimane	13.92	17.40	1.59	0.563	0.427
Larache	13.78	17.88	1.68	0.503	0.436
Settat	13.70	18.12	1.49	0.513	0.383
Khouribga	12.86	16.28	1.51	0.566	0.425
Meknès	12.85	16.17	1.54	0.488	0.664
Al Hocima	12.70	13.59	1.79	0.609	0.628
Oujda-Angad	12.66	16.90	1.27	0.609	0.628
Mediouna	11.93	17.78	1.06	0.619	0.731
Tétouan	11.04	14.55	1.32	0.554	0.378
Fès	10.66	16.89	0.94	0.599	0.753
Guelmim	10.37	12.80	1.34	0.599	0.716
Skhirate-Temara	10.26	15.90	1.11	0.594	0.620
Inezgane-Assilah	9.37	12.96	1.02	0.658	0.547
Tanger-Assilah	9.37	12.96	1.02	0.658	0.547
Beni Mellal	9.22	16.95	0.86	0.497	0.629
Agadir Ida ou Tanane	8.86	10.57	1.13	0.666	0.487
Marrakech	7.91	16.04	0.73	0.593	0.662
Tan-Tan	7.70	10.56	1.04	0.656	0.382
Nouaceur	7.19	13.04	0.62	0.600	0.742
Assa-Zag	*6.88*	*10.16*	*0.88*	*0.727*	*0.401*
Salé	6.45	10.88	0.68	0.663	0.451
Laayoune	*6.43*	*9.12*	*0.86*	*0.668*	*0.451*
Boujdour	*5.87*	*9.23*	*0.77*	*0.668*	*0.360*
Es-Smara	*4.74*	*7.45*	*0.57*	*0.692*	*0.874*
Mohammadia	4.28	9.15	0.33	0.673	0.836
Aousserd	*3.22*	*4.60*	*0.36*	*0.806*	*0.664*
Oued Ed-Dahab	*2.78*	*4.68*	*0.33*	*0.781*	*0.557*
Casablanca	2.73	7.09	0.18	0.762	—
Rabat	2.38	5.21	0.22	0.780	—

regions and that of the three sociologically similar regions to which they are compared, Chichaoua, Figuig, Taradounat (26.16). The ratio of difference between these two rates is approximately 5.) In other words, the probability of having to suffer from poverty or to be threatened by it is five times lower than for the sociologically similar regions taken as points of comparison.

The same conclusion is arrived at by studying the poverty severity index. The values of this index vary for the Saharan regions between 0.33 and 0.88. They are the lowest of Morocco, with the exception of Casablanca and Rabat. Those of the sociologically similar regions to which we compare the Saharan regions vary between 3.0 and 4.08. If an average value is taken for these rates, it can be seen that the Saharan provinces enjoy at least 15 times greater chance of being spared severe poverty than the sociologically similar provinces to which they are compared.

The values of the social and human development indices are also high for the Saharan regions. They vary between 0.668 and 0.806, i.e. better than Casablanca and Rabat for which the human development index is equal to 0.762 and 0.780, respectively. In this instance, there is no point in conducting a comparison between the Saharan regions and the three other sociologically similar regions taken as points of comparison in this research.

In fact, if one wanted to go into detail and analyse the variations of these indices for each commune, one would arrive at even more telling results. By way of example, let us stick to Oued Ed-Dahab–Lagouira and compare it to the second major economic hub of Morocco, i.e. Sous-Massa-Draa. The extreme values of poverty for the first are of 13.28 and 0.03, and for the second 60.26 and 3.20. This data is extracted from the major publication of the High Commission for Planning entitled *Pauvreté, développement human et social au Maroc/Poverty, human and social development in Morocco*. The reader may refer to page 23 for Oued Ed-Dahab and 24-30 for Sous-Massa-Draa.

The reader might think that the choice of Sous-Massa-Draa was made to support my thesis. To satisfy his/her curiosity, and show that I systematically apply the Popperian principle according to which one must always attempt to falsify assumptions rather than try to confirm them empirically, I refer to the data for the communes of the leading economic hub of Morocco, namely Greater Casablanca. In this case, the extreme values are greater than those for Oued Ed-Dahab, as they vary between 20.22 and 0.81. Let us point out that the gaps

Table 7.3: *Gives the values of all the indices for the communes of the Oued Ed-Dahab–Lagouira region*

Communal poverty, vulnerability and inequality indicators for human and social development

Province	Commune	Region : OUED ED-DAHAB–LAGOUIRA						
		Rate (%)		Index (%)			Communal development indices	
		Poverty	Vulnerability	Poverty severity	Inequality		Human	Social
Aousserd	Zoug	13.28	17.68	1.46	38.93		0.622	0.996
Aousserd	Tichla	11.35	16.22	1.47	35.99		0.667	0.964
Oued Ed-Dahab	Mijik	9.73	12.03	0.99	37.19		0.675	1.000
Aousserd	Agbouinite	8.00	10.66	1.01	25.37		0.698	1.000
Aousserd	Aousserd	5.73	7.98	0.63	45.22		0.588	0.773
Oued Ed-Dahab	Bir Anzarane	3.90	6.21	0.41	38.10		0.713	0.938
Oued Ed-Dahab	Dakhla (M)	3.07	5.19	0.37	44.19		0.743	—
Oued Ed-Dahab	Gleibat El Foula	2.39	4.42	0.29	30.19		0.724	0.949
Oued Ed-Dahab	Oum Dreyga	1.50	4.03	0.12	33.06		0.647	0.967
Aousserd	Lagouira (M)	0.95	1.65	0.08	35.73		0.740	—
Aousserd	Bir Gandouz	0.09	0.24	0.01	35.37		0.794	0.322
Oued Ed-Dahab	Imlili	0.04	0.26	0.00	33.82		0.772	0.352
Oued Ed-Dahab	El Argoub	0.03	0.21	0.00	35.48		0.814	0.493

Note: In this table, the sign — indicates that the urban commune or Other Urban Centre (AC) is not included in the communal social development index, as the index is being to the rural areas.

Source : Haut Commissariat au Plan (2004).

Map 1: *Map of poverty by commune*

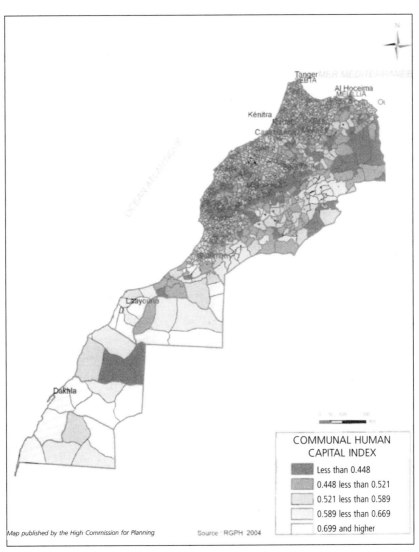

Map 2: *Map of human capital index by commune*

for Rabat, the political and administrative capital, vary between 27.32 and 0.20.

A systematic analysis of all the data for the communes of all regions of the Kingdom leads to the same conclusion: the gaps in the poverty index of Oued Ed-Dahab are lower than anywhere else.

The maps may be clearer indicators than statistics alone. They make it possible to take a rapid glance at all the communal variations in poverty.

So how can one explain the privileged situation of the Saharan region without consideration of the massive investment and redistribution policies of the Moroccan Government? Social and human development in the Sahara cannot be understood unless these are taken into account.

Let us continue our analyses by taking a look at longitudinal data on poverty. The information and studies of this issue were produced for the High Commission for Planning.

2/ EVOLUTION OF POVERTY AND REGIONAL COMPARISONS

The following graph [Figure 7.1] shows the evolution of relative poverty at the national level and in urban environments from 1985 to 1999. Starting from 13.8 and 26.7 in 1985, in urban and rural areas

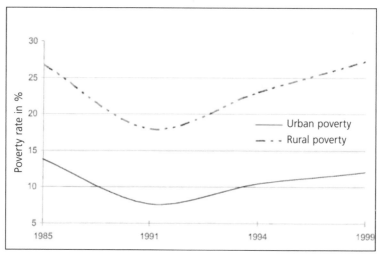

Figure 7.1: *Evolution in the rates of relative poverty from 1985 to 1999 according to residential area*

Source: High Commission for Planning (2004).

respectively, relative poverty saw a drop from that date and up to 1991, later reaching levels almost similar to those of 1999.

The moment relative poverty increases in both environments and in almost all the provinces of Morocco; it decreases, however, in the two Saharan regions. Only the region of Guelmim-Es-Smara registered a worsening level of relative poverty. The following graphs are eloquent in this respect. Instead of conducting a complete longitudinal study from 1985 to 1999, it suffices to focus attention on the period during which relative poverty saw net progression, corresponding to the second half of the 1990s.

Figure 7.2 clearly demonstrates that, while relative poverty in rural areas increased throughout Morocco, it decreased in the Saharan provinces, notably in Laayoune, Boujdour, Oued Ed-Dahab and Sakia El Hamra. Only the rural regions of Greater Casablanca were as immune as the Saharan regions. For reasons of completeness, it must be pointed out that the region of Guelmim Es-Smara showed a slight rise in relative poverty of 5%.

The same remarks can be made on the evolution of relative poverty in urban areas as depicted in figure 7.3. Even though it shows net progression in half of the regions of Morocco, on the other hand, it

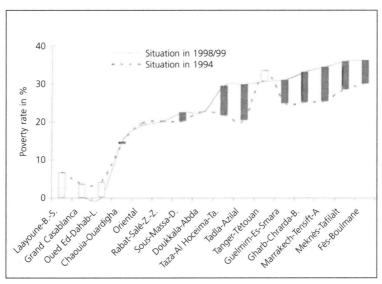

Figure 7.2: *Evolution in the rate of relative urban poverty per region from 1994 to 1998–99*

Source: High Commission for Planning (2004).

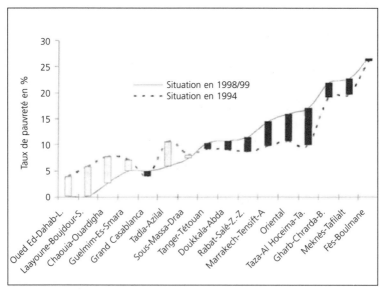

Figure 7.3: *Evolution in the rate of relative urban poverty per region from 1994 to 1998–99*

Source: High Commission for Planning (2004).

points to one of the strongest regressions in Oued Ed-Dahab Lagouira, Laayoune, Boujdour, Sahia El Hamra, and even Guelmim–Es-Smara.

What are the determinants of poverty? The answer to this question will be determined by the validity of the general thesis that has been subject to empirical test. These factors, human capital, related in particular to literacy rates, the socio-demographic structure, and the variables related to infrastructure, are all directly or indirectly linked to public investments and the transfer policies of the state. The low level of poverty in the Sahara is also explainable through wages policy; by increasing wage-levels twofold, through job creation generated by public investments, and the emphasis placed on the tertiary sector that I will discuss in due course.

The micro-economic and micro-sociological variables play only a very limited role in determining the various poverty thresholds reached by the communes and regions of the Sahara. If they played a more determinant role there than in the other regions of the Kingdom, one could assume that the inhabitants of these zones enjoy certain cultural or social specificities. However, this is definitely not the case. A culturalist assumption of this kind has no foundation whatsoever. We might even be tempted to assume the contrary for reasons stemming

134

from the nature of the traditional economic activities in these regions that are based more on livestock breeding and trade than agriculture, industry or services.

Any reduction in poverty will then be the expected or unexpected consequence of political decisions. The assumption according to which poverty in the Saharan regions is supposed to be the sole or principal effect of the aggregation of individual patterns of behaviour must be dismissed.

This applies to the macro-sociological phenomena as well as to the gross and net rates of illiteracy and schooling at the different levels investigated earlier. These changes cannot be explained only as the expected or unexpected consequences of public policies.

If the Saharan regions are more immune to poverty than most of the other regions of Morocco, if the human development thereof is comparatively better and no different than that of the most economically and socially developed regions, this is surely attributable to the efforts of the State and the positive discrimination policy conducted over the past three decades.

8

Marriage in the Sahara

Are Sahrawis really what some think they are? Do they really form self-contained groups, impermeable to others? Do they live cloistered in a desert closed to the rest of the world, as some firmly believe? And do these people in their presumed insularity practice wholly endogamous marriage, rejecting all marital alliance with "outsiders"? Do we have solid foundations for believing, as has been claimed, that marital exchange in the Sahara is limited to certain tribes and tribal fractions? If this is so, we can reasonably inquire into the particular nature of Sahrawi social structure, the rules that generated these people's closed social system and, correlatively, whether this population group is indeed fundamentally resistant to integration. However, there is reason to believe that the above claims are no more than hasty value-judgments, or components of unsound arguments aimed at justifying and rationalizing what are in fact pre-existing political opinions relative to the supposed irredentism of the Sahrawis and their seemingly appalling "psychology." This should become fully clear if we look at those claims, judgments and opinions in light of the facts.

The least objectionable, most obvious criterion for measuring a society's or group's degree of openness is the degree to which it accepts mixed marriage, whether the mix be ethnic, religious or social. Moreover, marriage is one of the most important indicators of social integration. First, it expresses the morphological dimension of integration: a society made up of groups that do not exchange men and women with each other is a closed society. In general, when the rate of this type of exchange between communities is low or non-existent, the ties *within* each of the communities is strong. Such a society, like caste societies, practices strict endogamy, but it is different from them on several points: a caste never corresponds to a specific territory, and it is occupationally homogeneous, contrary to a tribe, whose existence is inscribed within a given territory and which is made up of individuals of different socio-occupational statuses and amounts of power. Such closed societies exert strong pressure on their members to all behave in the same way, contrary to a society where mixed marriage is freely accepted and occurs frequently.

Second, given that a society and its social groups never grant individuals absolute freedom to marry as they like because marital union affects the very existence of the given group's organization and the organization of the society as a whole, marriage can be said to reflect (if not entirely) the normative dimension of integration. This is one reason that societies and communities impose strict rules, either implicit or explicit, written or oral, which individuals are expected to follow when choosing their spouse. This is widely confirmed by ethnological and sociological research.

In segmentary societies such as the traditional Sahrawi one, the rules governing marital alliance are known, and individuals are unlikely to depart from them. Those rules prescribe choosing one's spouse from one or another specific tribe or tribal fraction or, in the case of most Arab Sahrawi tribes, marrying one's parallel first cousin, specifically one's father's brother's daughter (*bint al-'amm*). This is what is commonly called preferred marriage among Arabs (Chelhod 1965). Anthropological studies, particularly those of the great Rguibat tribe, show that preferred marriage is relatively frequent; they also explain that the system of egalitarian marital alliances referred to in the literature actually corresponds to inequality, is rank and status hierarchies, and favours the development of alliance networks in struggles for power.[1]

1/ THE STUDY: DATA AND LIMITATIONS

The data in the sociological study I conducted do not allow us to descend to that level of ethnographic precision; we cannot use them to measure the salience of preferred marriage among Saharan Arabs or assess the difference between actual marriage behaviour and the ideal type. The study is based on marriage contracts that do not specify a filial tie (if any) between spouses—they are not required to by law. But what is lost in intensity is amply gained in extension. Anthropological studies generally go no further than analysing a few cases in great detail, whereas the corpus I used attains a dimension unknown in those works: nearly 30,000 marriages. The size of the study population in what is, as far as I know, a one-of-a-kind study allows for exhaustive variable cross tabulation and extremely fine multivariate analysis. The data allow for measuring all forms of homogamy and regional endogamy or homochtony. Social homogamy refers to marriages between individuals from the same social milieu. Regional endogamy, or homochtony, refers to spatial proximity between spouses' birthplaces. However, proximity between spouses' households of origin goes beyond geographical considerations. It is certainly not because individuals live especially close to each other that they marry. In fact, physical distance may reasonably be said to reflect social, ethnic, religious or occupational distance.

The essential question in this chapter is whether people born in the Sahara are becoming increasingly heterogamous or whether they remain strictly homogamous and indeed endogamous as in the past. To answer this question empirically is to come to understand that the populations that make up this region are opening up to external influences and gradually becoming integrated into Moroccan society as a whole. I will show that despite the colonial borders, Sahrawis' heterogamous marriages during the period of Spanish occupation were contracted exclusively with other Moroccans, specifically other Saharans. There are a few isolated cases of marriage to Mauritanians and foreigners, but the number is insignificant compared to other kinds of marital exchange. The importance and significance of this sociological datum should escape no one. First and foremost it should be heeded by the masters of the moment, who, in the silence of their studies, seek to map out abstract territorial borders rather than inquiring into the real life of populations.

Ideally, if the data had allowed, I would have focused this analysis on endogamy in the strict sense of the term. Unfortunately, determining each spouse's tribe of origin is an extremely delicate matter that would require an amount of labour no one is in a position to perform. Marriage contracts do not necessarily mention tribes; rather, the partial information obtained on the tribes that individuals belong to has been constructed using components of these contracts. There are gaps in the data that make it impossible to use the tribal membership variable systematically for the time being. In order to account for the specificity of Sahrawi tribe social structure, I will instead analyse the rates of increase in heterogamous marriage by residence zone; I will do so by cross-tabulating this variable with others.[2]

It must be specified that to test our fundamental hypothesis and rigorously measure heterogamy, it is not enough to analyse the development of the phenomenon in the Saharan regions; the phenomenon would also have to be studied in the general framework of Moroccan society as a whole, itself characterized by an extremely high rate of social, local and tribal homogamy. Regional and social homogamy are very common in Morocco. However, we do observe that this type of marriage is becoming less frequent as the society changes, as it modernizes. Emile Durkheim would surely have seen this phenomenon as clear evidence that the society was moving from mechanical to organic solidarity; in simpler if clumsier terms, this could be called the transition from a traditional to a modern society. In earlier times, marriages were contracted only between persons belonging to the same socio-occupational milieu. This type of homogamy still predominates in Morocco; it is also quite common in advanced industrial societies.[3]

In traditional Moroccan society, as in the Saharan tribes, choice of spouse follows other explicit though unwritten rules, rules that favour social or territorial endogamy. Their hold is loosening gradually, and exogenous unions are becoming slightly more common. A previous study of choice of spouse in Casablanca showed continuing high endogamy, despite the fact that this major city constitutes a relatively open social milieu characterized by a much more pronounced population mix than anywhere else in Morocco.[4]

Any interpretation of marriage in the Sahara must take account of these remarks and be attentive to local specificities. Though the figures indicate extremely clear trends, they are not enough to enable us to understand the significant sociological meaning of heterogamous marriage among this population. We need to take into account the strength of the tribal ties prohibiting heterogamy; also to keep in mind the demanding material conditions for getting married.

To test my general research hypothesis, we would also have to take into account another aspect of Sahrawi marriage. This study bears only on marriage in the Sahara, not on spouse choice among Sahrawis in general, some of whom live and marry in other Moroccan provinces.

In fact, we know that heterogamous marriage is relatively common in big cities like Casablanca, Marrakech, Rabat and Fès, though we do not know the exact number of such marriages. Inasmuch as I can trust my informers and my own experience, I am inclined to think that the vast majority of those unions are exogamous. Close study of all the "Adoulian" registers scattered throughout the kingdom would be a superhuman task requiring an incalculable amount of time and an army of research assistants; it is a task quite beyond my modest means.[5] But the high rate of exogamy for Sahrawis living outside the Sahara should be kept in mind while reading this chapter: the rate of increase of Sahrawi heterogamy is unquestionably higher than the study data show.

My research assistants and I systematically consulted all Adoulian registers containing marriage contracts and noted all information in them. All these contracts are handwritten. Anyone who has had the opportunity to decipher the handwriting of an "Adoul" or "clerk" of the Cadi can imagine the difficulties involved in amassing a corpus of documents. The list of variables in note 6 gives a clear idea of the information contained in the contracts.[6]

The aim was to cover the period from the early 1960s to 2007. Despite all my efforts and the precious assistance made available to me, I was not always able to gain access to all registers for every year. Some are missing. Moreover, the registers for the early years of the study period do not always have all the information found in more recent records, which are richer and more systematic in the sense that they more closely follow professional "Adoul" codes. Lastly, it should be noted that during the colonial period not all marriages involved a contract duly transcribed by the Cadi clerk. What was true for the other Moroccan regions holds for the Sahara: during the colonial period numerous marriages, especially rural ones, were made within the family, without any marriage document of any kind, in the presence of twelve witnesses who socially officialized and religiously blessed the ceremony and union by reading the opening passages of the Koran.

Data processing assistants were instructed to enter *all* the data contained in each register. To eliminate a major source of error, no coding was done while data was being entered.

Furthermore, to preclude all interpreting during the coding phase, coding was done by two persons only, including myself. When we had difficulty identifying a tribe or place of residence (usually rural), I relied on an informant originally from the great Rguibat tribe and intimately familiar with the Southern provinces.

2/ CHANGE IN REGIONAL ENDOGAMY RATES AND ITS MEANING

A reader contemplating Figure 8.1 could only conclude that regional endogamy in the Sahara fell quite markedly between 1947 and 2007. This holds for both men and women. The graph was constructed from a table cross-tabulating spouses' birth zones and marriage year, the latter recoded using five intervals. I distinguished three zones: what is commonly called Western Sahara, the other Saharan regions of southern Morocco, and all other regions of Morocco. The rare cases of marriage to foreigners (146 men and 40 women) were not taken into account.

We see that since the end of Spanish colonization—i.e., the first observation point on the x-axis: time—rates of endogamy have fallen by 95.6% for men and 92.1% for women, to respective lows of 50.3% for men and 53.1% for women. The rates were calculated by cross-tabulating spouses' respective birth zones. Let me repeat that to preclude all ambiguity, I distinguished between the former provinces colonized by Spain, that is, Western Sahara properly speaking; the other Saharan regions, some of which had been reintegrated earlier into Morocco (the case of Guelmim, Ifni, Tarfaya and Tan Tan); and Morocco's non-Saharan regions. All rate calculations concern Western Sahara only.

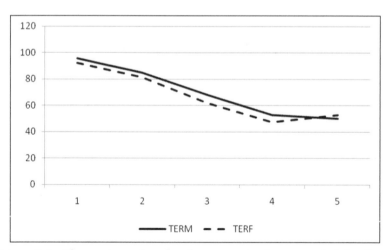

Figure 8.1: *Change in regional endogamy rates by sex and date of marriage*

Note: TERM = Regional Endogamy Rate, Men; TERF = Regional Endogamy Rate, Women

If, as the results of this data analysis clearly show, the regional endogamy rate fell by 45.3% for men and 39% for women, this is because social ties in the region have profoundly changed since 1975, when the borders between the Saharan provinces and the other regions of Morocco disappeared, opening the way for intensification of economic, social and domestic exchange. The frequency of ethnically and regionally homogamous marriages has greatly fallen in the last forty years, despite the strong social pressure that all social groups normally exert on their members to limit exogamy. Interestingly, Western Sahara in this respect is not very different from Casablanca, the great economic centre of Morocco (I refer here to data from a study done by one of my doctoral students in the late 1980s): the homogamy rate in Casablanca at that time was nearly 50% for men, 60% for women.[7]

The question raised by this change is, what are the regions and social characteristics of individuals who marry Sahrawis? We can examine those marital exchanges first at the general level, without taking into account the time variable. Once again, Western Sahara properly speaking (code 1) was distinguished from the Saharan regions that Morocco gained back before 1975 (code 3) and other regions of Morocco (code 2).

Not surprisingly, we observe a high regional homogamy rate, which can be read directly along the main diagonal of the exchange matrix. But this is not my immediate concern, since my aim is to analyse marital exchange.

Several methodologies can be used to study this matrix. The simplest is to analyse it in terms of percentages. First—and as we expected in fact—Saharans are much more likely to marry among themselves than to get married to individuals from other regions. 15% of Western Sahara Sahrawis marry women from other Saharan regions and only 12.4% marry women from other Moroccan regions (hereafter called Northern provinces to distinguish them from the Southern, i.e., Saharan, provinces). Men in Southern provinces other than Western Sahara are very nearly as likely as Sahrawis to choose their wives from among Western Sahara Sahrawi women rather than from among women native to their own region: 38.4% versus 41.2%. At the overall level, marital exchanges balance out due to marriage market mechanisms, mechanisms whose structure we do not really know.

It is worth noting the similarity of demographic distributions of men and women for the three birth zones. This point is crucial and needs to be explained. If we examine geographical distribu-

Table 8.1: *Marital exchange matrix*

			Wife's zone			Total
			1	2	3	
Husband's zone	1	N =	5,232	894	1,078	7,204
		% by husband's zone	72.6%	12.4%	15.0%	100.0%
		% by wife's zone	70.1%	11.5%	37.0%	39.7%
	2	N =	1,178	6,314	699	8,191
		% by husband's zone	14.4%	77.1%	8.5%	100.0%
		% by wife's zone	15.8%	81.3%	24.0%	45.1%
	3	N =	1,058	559	1,135	2,752
		% by husband's zone	38.4%	20.3%	41.2%	100.0%
		% by wife's zone	14.2%	7.2%	39.0%	15.2%
Total		N =	7,468	7,767	2,912	18,147
		% by husband's zone	41.2%	42.8%	16.0%	100.0%
		% by wife's zone	100.0%	100.0%	100.0%	100.0%

tion of the two sexes independently of exchanges occurring inside the matrix—in other words, if we study the marginal distributions of men and women across the three zones—we see that, with the exception of a few percentage points, they are identical for the two sexes. The respective figures for men are 39.7%, 45.1% and 15.2%; for women 41.2%, 42.8% and 16%. Since there is little difference between the two distributions, we might estimate that the margins impose no constraint on marital exchange. Had I found markedly different marginal distributions, this would have led me to suppose the existence of structural constraints that impacted heavily on the individuals in question.

We can see this more clearly if we imagine an unbalanced marriage market; i.e., with more men than women or vice versa. Balance has to be attained, either by opening up that market or forcing people to remain single. Demographers and sociologists are familiar with this problem, dubbed "marriage squeeze." It appears after particularly bloody wars which, by decimating the soldier population of men of marriageable age, leave behind a "surplus" of women of that same age.

Sociologists of social mobility work with a very similar phenomenon when analysing mobility tables that are almost identical to Table 8.1. They have termed this problem forced exchange mobility or structural mobility. The simplest case is massive rural exodus, which unbalances the given socio-occupational structure and "frees" millions of peasant children, in fact forcing them into occupational mobility: they are not free to remain in the countryside and practice their father's occupation.

It is perfectly reasonable to analyse Table 8.1 as if it were a mobility matrix. We can determine the degree of exchange among the three zones as if they were the socio-occupational categories of social mobility sociology. There are several types of mobility matrices; on this subject Boudon's synthesis is particularly useful (Boudon 1973b). Here I will use the Yasuda index, a means of calculating the distance between real table data and the data in a theoretical table constructed in this case using the hypothesis of statistical independence between spouses' birth zones. Theoretically, the value of this index is 0 when there is no exchange and 1 when exchange is maximal. For Table 8.1 the value is equal to 0.468,[8] indicating relatively high marital exchange among the three birth zones studied.

It may of course be claimed that the rate falls observed are likely to be due to the waves of migrants from Morocco's non-Saharan provinces who have chosen to settle in the Sahara since its reincorporation into Morocco. Couldn't marriages between new settlers and non-Sahrawis be what increased the heterogamy rate at a recent time in the study period? In fact, this argument is specious. It does not call into question the fundamental observation. First, we are analysing marriage rates for individuals born in the Sahara; no others were taken into account. Second, taking into account marriage year dispels any ambiguity. Third, analysing the same data by individuals' date of birth could either validate or invalidate the result. By analysing the ages of individual men and women born in the Sahara, we are able to clearly distinguish those born before 1975 from those born in or after that year, once again dispelling all ambiguity. Figure 8.2 below presents endogamy rate evolution by spouses' birth years.

The fourth figure is somewhat out of synchronization with the other three, for the simple reason that we do not have all the registers for men for this fourth age bracket or for women for the first two age brackets. In this case we have no more than 25 and 152 marriages, compared to the thousands of registered marriages for the other age brackets.

With the exception of this situation, the results of the data analysis—fairly complex, it should be remembered—obtained by

Men born before 1950
Women born before 1960

Men born before 1960
Women born before 1970

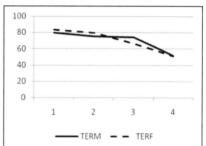

Men born before 1966
Women born before 1974

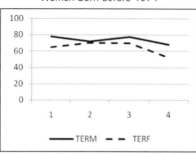

Men born before 1975
Women born after 1974

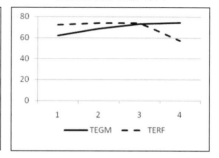

Men born after 1974 and Women born after 1974

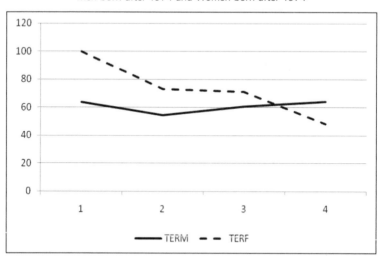

Figure 8.2: *Regional endogamy rates by spouses' birth years and birth zones*

Note: TERM = Regional Endogamy Rate, Men; TERF= Regional Endogamy Rate, Women

simultaneously cross-tabulating four variables, indicate a generalized fall in regional endogamy rates. But they have more to teach us, as follows:

1/ Overall, women's rates have fallen more markedly than men's. For men, the gap between highest and lowest endogamy rates is 30%, whereas for Saharan women it is 50%.

2/ The interaction effects that appear deserve particular attention. They are visible in the fact that the rate curves for spouses by birth year/age are dissimilar. These interaction effects mean that the endogamy rate varies simultaneously by husband's age and wife's age.

3/ Women's endogamy rate in the study's first age groups is higher than men's. At the end of the period studied, however, women's rates are lower than men's. This is to be interpreted as the effect of women's new modernity and their relative degree of openness to social groups other than their reference group. Women are no longer domestic priestesses charged with defending traditional values in the private sphere, tending its sacred hearth fires and socializing children into these values.

4/ At younger spouse ages, endogamy rates fall quite significantly. Young wives have particularly low homochtony rates. The interpretation given for women in 3/ seems to apply to the younger generations as well.

5/ The younger the wife, the less likely the husband is to have married endogamously. This is the result of the dual movement identified in the preceding points, which also applies to the converse statement:

6/ The younger the husband, the less likely the wife is to have married endogamously. It should be recalled that on average, the age at which men marry is ten years above the age at which women marry.

We reach the same conclusions if we submit the table data corresponding to Figure 8.2 to finer systematic statistical analysis, using variable association measures such as *phi*, the contingency coefficient or Cramer's V. Readers interested in such methodological considerations will find the contingency coefficient value table in the Appendix. For reasons of space, I have only made use of the values of this qualitative variable measure for each age group of the two spouses. To help readers grasp the entire set of changes in the values of this measure of endogamy strength, I have translated them graphically. The falling trend of contingency coefficient values for each male and female age group clearly indicates a marked decrease in endogamy.

These statements are corroborated by still more complex analyses that I have not reproduced here. We see exactly the same trends just brought to light when we study endogamy rates by spouses' birth year and year of marriage. To do so, I cross-tabulated five variables, recoded once again because of the weakness of certain boxes in the final matrix. Some exogamy rates are as high as 60%.

These results are explained by the social changes and transformations of the Saharan marriage market, a market whose real structure we do not actually know. Our study data do not allow for defining, measuring or analysing either supply or demand on this market; they only allow for observing the facts which I have here interpreted briefly. Sociologists would surely demand more, and that is understandable. But to move beyond what has already been determined would require a systematic use of the data that does not fit with our purposes here and is of interest only to the relevant specialists, i.e., demographers or sociologists of the family.

However, our data and our analyses of it can teach us still more. We see that, proportionally, the most intense marital exchange takes place between Western Sahara Saharans and Saharans of the other Southern provinces. This result confirms the deduction made at the end of the detailed study of Table 8.1. And an explanation for it is ready to hand: Saharans from these two major zones belong to tribes of similar structure; they share a history of several centuries and virtually identical cultures, despite a few local specificities. Socially, they are much more closely linked than is generally thought.

It will surely be remarked that our analyses lead us to conclusions of the sort that certain Saharans sense themselves or actually know. But it is one thing to have a dim, confused notion of something, another to demonstrate the soundness of that notion. Moreover, if we accept the obvious and admit that these populations all have many essential points in common, that they are in fact so similar that it is difficult to distinguish them from each other, it becomes impossible to understand how anyone could envisage splitting them into two entities. Decreeing a border between Western Sahara and the other Southern provinces would be sociologically absurd. The Saharans of Western Sahara feel this so strongly that they think of the other Saharans as part of their own family. The entire region could of course be remodelled to satisfy the separatist impulses, with a huge Saharan zone running from Tiznit to Lagouira. But then why stop there? The remodellers might go on to integrate the entire Sous-Massa-Draa region, then the southern zone of the High Atlas, and from one area to the next, all of Morocco would end up integrated into Western Sahara.

3/ TRENDS IN MARITAL EXCHANGE BY SOCIAL MILIEU

A person is always more likely to marry within his or her own social milieu than in any other, despite any change in social structure, despite increasing diversification of groups and milieus, and despite one's/the person's possible experience of social mobility. Such structural changes definitely attenuate social homogamy; they do not eliminate it. It is the same thing in all societies.

Studies of choice of spouse in industrial societies have shown that the strongest homogamy is among farmers and manual/service sector workers. It tends to decline among people in the more privileged groups. It is weakest in intermediate occupation groups such as tradespersons, office workers and especially managers. It is strongest in the very highest social strata. The relation between homogamy and social hierarchy is expressed by a curvilinear or "U" model. In fact, we can easily show that what accounts for this state of affairs is these societies' hierarchical structures and the distances separating the different social strata. Groups in the middle of this hierarchy have the lowest homogamy rates. We cannot expect to find intense marital exchange between the two social groups at the extremities of the social ladder. These theorems can be deduced automatically from the axiomatics of a simple macro-structural theory, as Blau suggests (1977), in developing a seminal idea of Simmel (1908).

Is this the way things are in the Sahara? Does the regional endogamy of Sahrawis change by their social-occupational status? Are some social categories more exogamous than others? This question can be answered using simultaneous analysis of Sahrawi endogamy rates by socio-occupational status and marriage year.

The first observation to be made is that regional endogamy rates are systematically falling in all categories. There is no exception to this rule despite minor fluctuations by year. Moreover, the shape of the fall is practically the same for all categories. It can be described by a hyperbolic function equation, and this implies the existence of an asymptote,

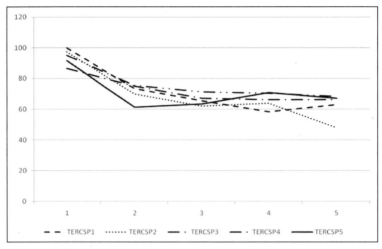

Figure 8.3: *Change in regional endogamy rates by marriage year and socio-occupational category*

Notes: CSP1 = category encompassing farmers, service sector workers, manual/blue-collar workers, drivers; CSP2 = military personnel; CSP3 = employees, office workers and mid-level civil servants; CSP4 = trades and craftspersons; CSP5 = liberal professions, senior managers, engineers, technicians, and students.

meaning that the exogamy rate for each social category would in all likelihood reach a threshold below which it could no longer fall. We see that with the exception of the second social category, where the lowest rate is 48% (it will be recalled that this category is made up primarily of military personnel), all social strata have an endogamy rate around 62%.

The possible existence of a threshold is of particular interest to sociologists and demographers, who are likely to inquire whether, below a certain homogamy threshold, the existence of certain groups is threatened. In order to answer this question we would have to construct simulation models; these would allow for detailed examination of the conditions in which changes in homogamy rates transform group social composition and the relations among those groups. Such simulation models would be similar to those proposed by Thomas Schelling (1978) for studying the effects of changing critical mass.

Marital exchange as practised by the Saharan population does not seem to correspond to the standard model identified for industrial societies. It follows a different logic, that of societies in which women used to dominate in the private sphere, possessing nearly absolute power over the household economy and reigning over child socialization, but where very recently they have begun to be schooled, are now timidly entering the job market, and assuming an increasingly sizeable proportion of the roles traditionally reserved for men in both the public

Table 8.2: *Husband's and wife's socio-occupational categories*

			Wife's occupation				Total
			0	1	2	3	
Husband's occupation	1	N =	3696	86	402	73	4257
		% by husband's occupation	86.8%	2.0%	9.4%	1.7%	100.0%
		% by wife's occupation	27.8%	28.6%	17.2%	10.5%	25.6%
	2	N =	1728	35	234	76	2073
		% by husband's occupation	83.4%	1.7%	11.3%	3.7%	100.0%
		% by wife's occupation	13.0%	11.6%	10.0%	10.9%	12.4%
	3	N =	4444	89	1102	329	5964
		% by husband's occupation	74.5%	1.5%	18.5%	5.5%	100.0%
		% by wife's occupation	33.4%	29.6%	47.1%	47.1%	35.8%
	4	N =	2355	45	375	114	2889
		% by husband's occupation	81.5%	1.6%	13.0%	3.9%	100.0%
		% by wife's occupation	17.7%	15.0%	16.0%	16.3%	17.3%
	5	N =	1092	46	228	106	1472
		% by husband's occupation	74.2%	3.1%	15.5%	7.2%	100.0%
		% by wife's occupation	8.2%	15.3%	9.7%	15.2%	8.8%
Total		N =	13315	301	2341	698	16655
		% by husband's occupation	79.9%	1.8%	14.1%	4.2%	100.0%
		% by wife's occupation	100.0%	100.0%	100.0%	100.0%	100.0%

Note: 0 = women without a paid occupation/non-working women; 1 = low socio-occupational category made up of blue-collar/manual and service workers; 2 = intermediate category made up of office workers, civil servants, trades- and crafts-persons; 3 = high category made up of managers, senior managers and the liberal professions.

and private spheres. Moreover, the intensity of the relation between husband's and wife's occupations is low. This is probably explained by the as yet high rate of non-working women/women in the home. Table 8.2, which cross-tabulates spouses' occupations, is quite clear on this point.

Though significant, the relation between these two variables is weak: the value of the contingency coefficient is 0.146. In the Sahara, social homogamy is so low that is it difficult to compare it to what we observe in societies hierarchically organized by occupation and the other stratifying criteria. And in this connection the Sahara is hardly different from the other regions of Morocco, above all Casablanca in the 1990s, where approximately the same rates of same-occupation spouses were found. But it is likely that in the future this region and the rest of Morocco will experience the trend expressed by the main hypothesis of convergence theory; i.e., convergence toward the industrial and post-industrial society model.

CONCLUSION

Although it hardly seems necessary to review or comment on the simple propositions established in this chapter, they can be meaningfully summarized. We are witnessing the gradual social integration of Sahrawis into Moroccan society as a whole, a development which, as far as I know, could not have been predicted, a development whose intensity no one foresaw. The number of marital exchanges is so high, and that exchange is so intense that we cannot be indifferent to this phenomenon. No one can fail to see it. The fact is that this social bond has been patiently woven by individual wills. It is entirely independent of institutional actors. To destroy it would constitute a detrimental attack against the freedom of men and women who have shown themselves willing to share the same future.

This is a modest conclusion to a research study that should be pursued. Will I be able to find the information that is missing for certain years? Shall I be able to fill in the considerable information gaps on spouses' tribal membership? Will I have the time needed to study all aspects of marriage in the Sahara?

APPENDIX TO CHAPTER 8

Though relatively simple, these statistics are instructive. They teach us that contrary to what is claimed, there is strong inequality between Sahrawi men and women when it comes to marriage—practically the same inequality as that observed for the rest of Morocco. First, the average age at which women marry in the Sahara is sharply below the average age at which men marry. Second, as age increases women become much less likely than men to marry—as is clearly shown by the fact that the standard deviation value for age distributions for women at time of marriage is much lower than the corresponding standard deviation value for men. The probability of a woman marrying at age 30 is low—equal to 0.22—whereas at the same age the probability of a man marrying is 0.58: 2.7 times higher than for a woman. It is true that divorced women in the Sahara frequently remarry, and this most likely raises less of a problem there than in the other regions of Morocco. But it does not explain the demographic characteristics of the Saharan population. For comparison purposes, we can cite the difference between men's and women's ages on first marriage for Morocco as a whole: 7 years. Moreover, Moroccan women's age on first marriage is currently 26. However, it is important to keep in mind the difference between average marriage age of the individuals studied here and first-marriage age.

Table 8.3: *Analysis of age distributions for men and women at time of marriage*

		Husband's marriage age	Wife's marriage age
N	Valid	25.926	25.926
	Missing	3.183	3.183
Average		34.7558	25.7618
Mean		32.0000	24.0000
Mode		30.00	22.00
Standard variation		11.29054	8.13944
Variance		127.476	66.251
Skewness		1.645	1.416
Standard deviation of skewness		.015	.015
Kurtosis		3.319	3.668
Standard deviation of Kurtosis		.030	.030

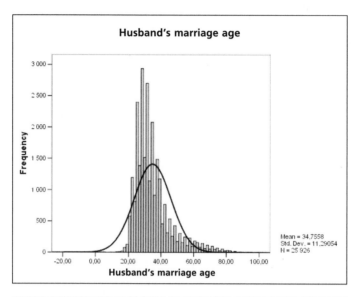

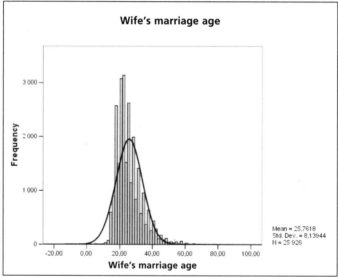

Figure 8.4: *Distribution of spouses' marriage age*

Table 8.1: *Contingency coefficient values for tables on spouses' birth zones and birth years*

Husband's birth year	Wife's birth year			Value	Significance
1	1	Nominal by nominal	Contingency coefficient	.595	.000
		Valid N per box		999	
	2	Nominal by nominal	Contingency coefficient	.443	.000
		Valid N per box		784	
	3	Nominal by nominal	Contingency coefficient	.466	.000
		Valid N per box		214	
	4	Nominal by nominal	Contingency coefficient	.470	.000
		Valid N per box		113	
2	1	Nominal by nominal	Contingency coefficient	.650	.000
		Valid N per box		661	
	2	Nominal by nominal	Contingency coefficient	.617	.000
		Valid N per box		1713	
	3	Nominal by nominal	Contingency coefficient	.586	.000
		Valid N per box		701	
	4	Nominal by nominal	Contingency coefficient	.480	.000
		Valid N per box		459	
3	1	Nominal by nominal	Contingency coefficient	.601	.000
		Valid N per box		208	
	2	Nominal by nominal	Contingency coefficient	.587	.000
		Valid N per box		1500	
	3	Nominal by nominal	Contingency coefficient	.587	.000
		Valid N per box		1101	
	4	Nominal by nominal	Contingency coefficient	.524	.000
		Valid N per box		1065	
4	1	Nominal by nominal	Contingency coefficient	.578	.000
		Valid N per box		88	
	2	Nominal by nominal	Contingency coefficient	.564	.000
		Valid N per box		952	
	3	Nominal by nominal	Contingency coefficient	.576	.000
		Valid N per box		1553	
	4	Nominal by nominal	Contingency coefficient	.548	.000
		Valid N per box		2975	
5	1	Nominal by nominal	Contingency coefficient	.626	.003
		Valid N per box		25	
	2	Nominal by nominal	Contingency coefficient	.574	.000
		Valid N per box		152	
	3	Nominal by nominal	Contingency coefficient	.524	.000
		Valid N per box		276	
	4	Nominal by nominal	Contingency coefficient	.495	.000
		Valid N per box		2087	

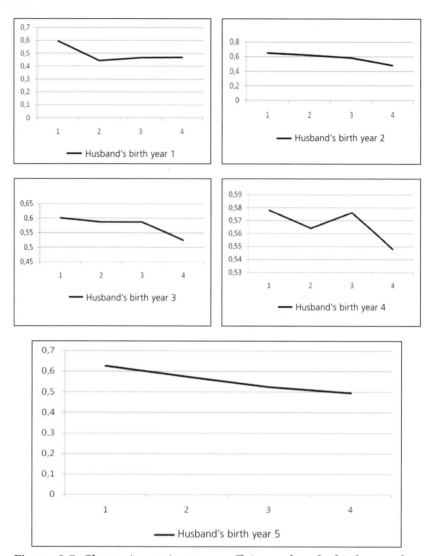

Figure 8.5: *Change in contingency coefficient values for birth zones by spouses' birth years*

The continuously falling contingency coefficient values for each of the male and female age groups clearly indicates that endogamy has greatly decreased. This conclusion, deduced by analysing the measure of dependence between spouses' birth zones, corresponds to and corroborates the conclusions reached by simple study of the percentages.

NOTES

1. See Caratini (1985, 1989 and 1995).

2. I constructed the following variables: marriage year, marriage month, marriage register page, marriage locale, identification of the husband, husband's birth year, husband's birthplace, husband's tribe, husband's occupation, husband's address, second identification of the husband, husband's mother's name, identification of the wife, wife's birth year, wife's birthplace, wife's tribe, wife's address, second identification of the wife, wife's mother's name, dowry (money), dowry (in kind). Furthermore, to control the quality of my research assistants' work, each was given an identification number so I could discuss their entries with them if necessary.

3. The studies in this area are too numerous to cite. The reader may consult the conclusions of the first study of spouse choice (Girard 1964), then supplement them with the work of Bozon and Héran (1987).

4. The study referred to was done in the framework of a thesis written and examined under my direction and published by Aboumalek (1994).

5. The registers that furnished the data for the study fall under the jurisdiction of the Moroccan justice administration; specifically, the equivalent of the county court. These registers contain more than marriage contracts. Each marriage contract was drawn up by two Adouls or clerks of the Cadi, the judge in charge of official personal matters (Moudawana).

6. Spouses' birth and marriage years were coded by intervals to ensure that the data tables contained large subsamples; meanwhile we were careful to respect the date marking the end of Spanish colonization: 1975. Marriage date was coded using five intervals: husband's birth year was also coded using five intervals, men born before 1948, between 1949 and 1958, between 1959 and 1964, between 1965 and 1974, and lastly men born in 1975 or later. For wife's birth year I coded using four intervals but starting ten years later than for men: women born before 1958, between 1959 and 1968, between 1969 and 1974, and in 1975 or later. In the Sahara as elsewhere, wives tend to be younger than their husbands.

7. See Aboumalek 1994, particularly pp. 99–103.

8. The Yasuda index is calculated using the formula below, which encompasses theoretical hypotheses related to the specificity of a mobility matrix. The formula is a convenient means of calculating the index value for any n-by-n matrix.

$$\left[\sum_{i=1}^{i=n}\min(n_{i.},n_{.i}) - \sum_{i=1}^{i=n}n_{ii}\right] / \left[\sum_{i=1}^{i=n}\min(n_{i.},n_{.i}) - \sum_{i=1}^{i=n}(n_{i.} \times n_{.i}/N)\right]$$

where $n_{i.}/n_{i.}$ and $n_{.i}/n_{.i}$ are the row and column marginal effects and N is sample size.

9

Modernization Processes and Social Movements

Alexis de Tocqueville's celebrated theory of revolutions and social movements as developed in *The Ancien Régime and the French Revolution* is well known. In Book 3, Chapter IV, the author offers the following concise account:

> *It is not always when things are going from bad to worse that revolutions break out. On the contrary, it more often happens that when a people which has put up with an oppressive rule over a long period without protest suddenly finds the government relaxing its pressure, it takes up arms against it. Thus the social order overthrown by a revolution is almost always better than the one immediately preceding it, and experience teaches us that, generally speaking, the most perilous moment for a bad government is one when it seeks to mend its ways. Only consummate statecraft can enable a King to save his throne when after a long spell of oppressive rule he sets to improving the lot of his subjects. Patiently endured so long as it seemed beyond redress, a grievance comes to appear intolerable once the possibility of removing it crosses men's minds* (pp. 176–77).

All the specialists on revolution and social movements have considered this argument, criticized it or attempted to test it and seeing how it holds up in relation to socio-historical facts. I have also devoted an essay to explaining the principles and social mechanisms it involves.[1]

In this chapter I would like to use Tocqueville's analyses to shed light on social movements in Morocco, particularly in the Saharan regions. Obviously the two sets of social and political contexts—that of Ancient Régime France and the one we are directly interested in here—are different. But a theory is only valid if it can explain several sets of similar phenomena. Tocqueville knew this and was always careful to make comparisons. He sought to account not merely for the French Revolution but all collective action that unfolds in time over several stages, from expressions of discontent to mobilizations against the political or social order in the aim of realizing the public good. And he was consistently concerned to analyse the vast social and political modernization processes we are interested in here.

The Tocquevillian hypothesis we will test is that the economic and social modernization experienced in Morocco and the Saharan provinces, the unprecedented liberalization process and degree of political liberty citizens now enjoy, the excessive expectations those same citizens have of the "demiurge or creator state" when it comes to solving their problems, have to be taken into account if we want to understand why interest in revolt is spreading among Moroccan young people, a social group that has of course enjoyed significant advantages but that is also tormented by uncertainty about the future.[2]

The first part of this chapter presents modernization indicators in the Saharan provinces as compared to the other regions of Morocco. The second part provides an analysis of certain social movements and offers a possible explanation of them in light of the results of the first part—it is more an outline than a fully developed theory, which would have required a detailed study.

The modernization indicators concern demographic change, universal schooling, urbanization, service sector development, consumption, the spread of certain types of business and state bureaucracy organization, communications, and democratization of the political sphere. Data is available only for certain of these indicators, and information on the social movements of interest to us here are unfortunately fewer still. This will therefore not be a systematic study, which would have demanded much richer socio-economic and political data and more substantial analyses of mobilization mechanisms, which will be indicated only briefly. The focus here is on the essential.

1/ ECONOMIC INTEGRATION OF THE SAHARA AND MODERNIZATION INDICATORS

A/ The Weight of Numbers: Demographic Change and Pressure on the Labour Market

We begin by analysing population developments in the six Saharan provinces of Boujdour, Aousserd, Laayoune, Es-Smara, Oued Ed-Dahab and Assa Zag over the last census period. This population grew at a much faster annual average rate than the nation as a whole: 5% versus 1.4%. The difference is partially explained by fertility rates for the provinces, which in 2004 reached 3.4 per woman of child-bearing age in Oued Ed-Dahab, 3.1 in Es-Smara and Boujdour, 2.9 in Assa Zag and 2.6 in Laayoune, whereas the national rate did not exceed 2.5. The gap between the two rates is also explained by the Moroccan government policy of decentralizing administrative services and increasing the autonomy of the Saharan provinces. This development created major social and economic infrastructure needs which in turn entailed considerable investment by the state and private economic actors. The state's policy may be seen in statistics on current levels of infrastructure coverage compared to the national average.

Analysing the demographic data by age bracket brings to light the existence of a demographic transition in the Saharan provinces,[3] a development signalled by the fall in proportion of children under 15 between 1994 and 2004 (from 36.4% to 32.7%) and the rise in the proportion of persons aged 15–59 (57.9% to 63.3%).

The percentage of individuals aged 60 and over remains low in the Sahara, at 3.8%, whereas for the national population the figure is 8%.

The most important conclusion to be drawn from these statistics is that demographic pressure on the labour market is greater in the

Table 9.1: *Population change in the Saharan provinces and Morocco, 1982–2004*

	1994	2004	1982/1994	1994/2004
Saharan provinces	238,926	389,151	−3.5	5.0
Morocco	26,073,717	29,891,708	2.1	1.4
(1)/(2) in %	0.9	1.3		

Source : Haut Commissariat au Plan

Table 9.2: *Population growth by major age group*

	1994				2004			
	0/14 years	15/59 years	60 years and +	Total	0/14	15/59	60 and +	Total
Saharan provinces	38.4	57.9	3.7	100.0	32.7	63.3	3.9	100.0
Morocco	37.0	55.9	7.1	100.0	31.3	60.7	8.0	100.0

Source : Haut Commissariat au Plan

Sahara than in the nation at large: 63.3% of the Saharan population is of legal working age, a figure significantly higher than the 60.7% for the nation as a whole, and a point to be kept in mind with regard to the problem of unemployment.

The Saharan region has of course become much more urbanized than all other Moroccan provinces, as a few figures amply indicate. From 1982-1994, the growth rate for the urban population in the Sahara rose as high 83.16%, as opposed to 53.74% for Morocco as a whole. The 1994-2004 rate was nearly 43%, whereas for the country as a whole it was 22.62%. These figures indicate a massive rural exodus within the Sahara. Certain Saharan regions lost nearly all of their rural residents. The massive exodus, which transformed the socio-occupational structure of the Saharan provinces, has raised considerable economic and social problems for the government and local authorities, problems that require policy treatment.

B/ Basic Infrastructure
Since 1975, public investment in basic infrastructure has been so great and varied that it deserves to be presented in much greater detail than is possible in the scope of this chapter. Before moving on to the essential, it is important at least to mention the road network, for example, which grew spectacularly from 1350 km of paved roadway and 850 km of dirt roads to 9505 km of official roadway, 3379 km of which are paved; also the building of airport and seaport infrastructure, which opened up the region, connecting it to the more developed areas of the kingdom and to the rest of the world.

Living conditions and standards of living in the southern provinces differ significantly from the national averages.

68.2% of urban households in Morocco own their home. In Aousserd the figure is as high as 71.6%, but in Laayoune it is barely

Table 9.3: *Home ownership and access to basic infrastructure*

	% of households that own their home	% of households connected to the drinking water system	% of households with electricity	% of households connected to the sewer system	% of households with telephone	% of households with a cell phone
Aousserd	71.6	35.4	75.9	29.2	10.4	45.6
Oued Ed-Dahab	44.5	61.3	77.3	43.6	10.1	68.2
Boujdour	64.9	33.0	85.1	0.0	7.5	63.8
Laayoune	37.2	69.8	93.2	60.5	15.6	74.6
Assa Zag	52.8	76.3	78.6	2.5	18.5	53.6
Es-Smara	46.5	68.5	92.7	62.3	13.7	68.1
Morocco	68.2	57.5	71.6	48.6	14.4	60.6

Source : *Recensement Général, 2004*, Haut Commissariat au Plan.

37.2%. With the exception of Aousserd, southern province levels are all lower than the national average. It is worthwhile recalling that from 1976-2006, implementation of the housing policy for the provinces led to the construction of 100,000 new housing units.

The percentage of Saharan province households connected to the drinking water system is sharply higher than the national average of 47.5%. Only Boujdour (35.4%) and Aousserd (33%) fall below that average. Such results obviously required implementing water resource allocation programmes in regions characterized by unfavourable natural conditions.

Electrification rates are greater for the Saharan provinces than the nation at large, ranging from 93.2% in Laayoune to 75.9% in Aousserd, while the national average is 71.6%.

Sewer system coverage varies across the Sahara. While the populations of Laayoune and Es-Smara are better covered than the nation as a whole— respective figures of 60.5%, 62.3% versus 48.6%—the problem remains for Boujdour (0%), Assa Zag (2.5%) and Aousserd (29.2%). These sharp inequalities are clearly due to the fact that population density in the last-named provinces is low and the provinces themselves, namely Aousserd and Assa Zag, were created only recently.

Telephone access in the Saharan provinces also varies considerably. While Oued Ed-Dahab and Laayoune have good cell phone coverage, the other provinces do not differ much on this point from the national average. The same is true for fixed telephone lines: the national average proportion of households with a telephone is 14.4%, while in the provinces it ranges from 7.5% (Boujdour) to 18.5% (Assa Zag).

These data on basic infrastructure are presented in Table 9.3.

C/ Development of Gross School Enrolment

I have already analysed literacy and school enrolment rates in two of the preceding chapters, but it is useful to recall here some fundamental facts on the spread of schooling relevant to the later discussion of unemployment and social movements. The earlier chapters clearly presented efforts by the government in this part of the country to eradicate illiteracy and increase enrolment above national levels. (Gross enrolment is the ratio between number of pupils at a given school level and number of individuals whose age corresponds to the official age for schooling at that level. Official primary school age, for example, is 6 to 11, but there can easily be children over 11 enrolled in primary school. This explains why in some cases the figure exceeds 100%.)

Table 9.4: *Development of gross school enrolment rates in the Saharan provinces by education-level age group, 1994–2004*

Age group	1994		2004	
	Saharan provinces	Morocco	Saharan provinces	Morocco
6–11 years old	90.8	73.2	115.4	113.1
12–14	65.1	45.1	91.7	60.3
15–17	29.6	21.6	47.5	31.2
6–17	71.2	53,9	95,6	78,0

Source: Rates calculated using figures from the *Annuaires Statistiques* of the Haut Commissariat au Plan

Gross enrolment rates in the Saharan provinces do seem to show considerable improvement in school enrolment for all educational levels. The gross primary school enrolment rate reached 115.4% in 2004, as opposed to 90.8% in 1994. Growth was even higher for enrolment in the Moroccan equivalent of middle school, rising from 65.1% in 1994 to 91.7% in 2004. For what is called "qualifying" high school, enrolment percentages in the Saharan provinces rose 18 points, while the national average over the same period rose barely 10.

Overall, from 1994 to 2004 the combined primary and secondary school enrolment rate rose from 71.2% to 95.6% for the Sahara versus 53.9% to 78% for Morocco as a whole.

The number of children attending primary school in the Saharan provinces rose 72.9% over those years while rising 38.9% in Morocco as a whole.

Table 9.5: *Characteristics of public primary schooling supply*

		Teachers (1)	Classrooms (2)	School pupils (3)	(3)/(1)	(3)/(2)
Saharan provinces	1994	942	552	32,019	34	58
	2004	1761	987	55,364	31	56
	+ %	86.9	78.8	72.9		
All Morocco	1994	98,487	66,838	2,769,323	28	41
	2004	135,663	89,813	3,846,950	28	43
	+ %	37.7	34.4	38.9		

Source: Annuaires statistiques, Haut Commissariat au Plan

These improvements were due to government efforts to strengthen school infrastructure, efforts materialized in part by the construction of 987 classrooms since 1975. From school year 1993–1994 to school-year 2003–2004, the number of classrooms grew 78.8% in the provinces as against only 34.4% in the nation at large.

The same observation holds for teaching staff, which from 1994–2004 grew by 86.9% in the Sahara versus an increase of 37.7% at the national level.

Though growth was slower at middle school level, the difference between the provinces and the country as a whole was still significant. The middle school teaching staff grew by 37.7% in the Saharan provinces, by only 15.6% for the country at large. There was a similar difference between classroom number growth: 34.4% versus 27.6%

Another factor that reflects the royal government's efforts in the area of education is population structure by education level. All the southern provinces have lower illiteracy rates than the national average of 43%. The best performances are in Laayoune (27.7%) and Es-Smara (33.3%). This observation is corroborated if we consider population structure by education level: in Oued Ed-Dahab the proportion of persons aged 10 and over with secondary education is 61.2%, in Laayoune it is 63%, and in Es-Smara 56.7%, as opposed to 49.5% in the nation as a whole.

The same can be observed for higher education, with the exception of Aousserd and Boujdour, where rates are below the national average.

Another characteristic of the southern provinces that may be considered an integration factor is the proportion of the population speaking Arabic and French. According to the 2004 census, the figures

Table 9.6: *Characteristics of public middle school supply*

		Teachers (1)	Classrooms (2)	School pupils (3)	(3)/(1)	(3)/(2)
Saharan provinces	**1994**	550	262	9,943	18	38
	2004	931	440	20,563	22	47
	+%	37.7	34.4	38.9		
All Morocco	**1994**	47,760	20,297	863,099	18	43
	2004	55,202	25,889	1,134,223	21	44
	+%	37.7	27.6	31.4		

Source : *Annuaires statistiques* of the Haut Commissariat au Plan

Table 9.7: *Population 10 years old and over by education level and province*

	All levels			
	Preschool	Primary/ secondary	Higher education	Illiteracy rates
Oued Ed-Dahab	3.9	61.2	4.9	29.7
Aousserd	6.6	51.5	2.2	42.5
Boujdour	4.6	51.4	3.6	40.3
Laayoune	3.7	63.0	5.1	27.7
Assa Zag	2.9	49.4	4.8	42.4
Es-Smara	4.5	56.7	5.1	33.3
All Morocco	2.7	49.5	5.0	43.0

Source: *Recensement Général 2004* [Census], Haut Commissariat au Plan

Table 9.8: *Languages spoken by province*

	Arabic	Arabic and French	Other foreign languages
Oued Ed-Dahab	19.6	38.1	12.6
Aousserd	26.6	24.4	6.5
Boujdour	24.2	27.6	7.8
Laayoune	18.7	40.1	13.4
Assa Zag	15.4	30.7	11.4
Es-Smara	20.7	35.4	10.6
All Morocco	17.3	30.3	9.4

Source: *Recensement Général 2004* [Census], Haut Commissariat au Plan

are 40.1% for Laayoune, 38.1% for Oued Ed-Dahab and 35.4% for Es-Smara, as opposed to 30.4% for Morocco at large. The following table, which also indicates percentages of individuals speaking other foreign languages, shows that people in the Sahara are generally more likely to speak French and Arabic than people in the nation as a whole. It is important to note that Arabic here refers to knowledge of the literary language, not a dialect.

D/ Employment and Unemployment
The following discussion is limited to certain specificities of the labour market and unemployment in the Saharan regions compared to the rest of Morocco.

From 2000 to 2005 the working population in the southern provinces rose annually on average by 1.4%, as opposed to a 2.2% average
annual increase in the nation as a whole. If we consider the structure
of the working population during the last six years we see a disparity
between the southern provinces and the nation.

The weight of the service sector in the labour market is a major
indicator of economic modernization. In the Saharan provinces, the
service sector is the main source of employment, responsible for 60%
of total available jobs. For the nation as a whole, on the other hand,
agriculture is the first job-creating sector, responsible on average for

Table 9.9: *Employment indicators for the southern provinces and Morocco at large*

	2000	2001	2002	2003	2004	2005
Southern Provinces						
"Activity" rate	43.2	44.2	46.4	42.3	42.2	41.4
Unemployment rate	25.2	18.5	20.9	21.2	20.9	18.3
Working population	139,903	157,849	166,275	148,272	154,692	147,727
Working population by sector (%)						
agriculture	23.1	26.4	25.3	24.1	26.8	19.9
industry	7.2	6.5	7.2	7.4	6.2	6.8
construction	7.4	7.9	9.8	8.9	8.2	10.2
services	62.1	59.2	57.6	59.5	58.8	62.8
other	0.2	—	0.1	0.1	—	0.3
National						
"Activity" rate	52.9	51.3	50.7	51.9	52.4	52.6
Unemployment rate	13.6	12.5	11.6	11.9	11.4	10.8
Working population	8,891,107	8,954,555	9,176,316	9,483,767	9,821,897	9,913,296
Working population by sector (%)						
agriculture	45.1	43.5	43.1	46.2	45.8	45.4
industry	13.4	13	13.4	12.8	12.7	12.4
construction	6.2	6.7	7	6.6	6.7	7.1
services	35.2	36.7	36.4	34.3	34.7	35
other	0.1	0.1	0.1	0.1	0.1	0.1

Source: *Enquêtes Emploi* survey, Haut Commissariat au Plan

45% of jobs whereas services represent only 35% of jobs. In other words, the service sector in the Sahara is nearly twice the size of the service sector in the nation at large.

From 2000-2005, the unemployment rate in the southern provinces was almost twice that of the nation at large: 25.2% versus 13.6% in 2000, 18.3% versus 10.8% in 2005. However, these figures also show that unemployment in both the provinces and the nation altogether fell sharply during this period.

From 2000–2005, the "activity" rate [= ratio of number of "active persons"—employed or actively seeking employment—to the entire population] in the southern provinces fell from 43.2% to 41.4%. The year 2002 was marked by a considerable rise in this rate, to 46.4%, while at the national level it stagnated: estimated at 52.9% in 2000, it was at 52.6% in 2005, falling to 50.7% in 2002—the opposite of what occurred in the southern provinces that year.

Recalling these characteristics of labor market structure and growth, along with the unemployment rate, which remains high despite its notable recent fall, is useful for the following analysis of social movements.

2/ MODERNIZATION AND SOCIAL MOVEMENTS

Social and political demonstrations by young people in Morocco are common and have been for several years. There has been as yet no serious, systematic study of them. There are not even any public statistics on them. During recent years, on Tuesdays and Wednesdays when the parliament is in session, sit-ins are staged by unemployed university graduates in front of the Moroccan parliament. The sit-ins have become a tradition and even a curiosity for onlookers, especially tourists, who pass in front of the heavy ochre and beige building that houses the national representative body so they can take in the fine view of the grand boulevard designed by Maréchal Lyautey's architect, Prost. The police are present and observe the proceedings from a certain distance, but they have not once in the last decade moved in on the demonstrators, who, for their part, wave their banners and occasionally make themselves heard, carefully choosing their chants, always rhymed, always somewhat caustic, hoping to attract their political representatives' attention to their predicament. The press, in any case, is no longer interested in them and give them no coverage, not even a back-page mention.

The same media take quite a different attitude to demonstrations in the Sahara. From the moment the country opened itself to democratic procedures and the citizens began to feel the unprecedented wind of freedom, youth demonstrations in the Saharan provinces have been receiving intense coverage in the national press, though once again, the number of demonstrations is no higher there than in other parts of the country. On some days the Saharan demonstrators get the honours of the front page, and journalists have even been known to echo their secessionist slogans—which in earlier times would have incurred a trial and certain jail sentence. The current understanding seems to be that all citizens now have the right to express their views freely, even extremist views, even views that call into question the inviolable principle of the nation's territorial integrity.

We are no more richly endowed with statistics on political demonstrations by human rights organizations in southern Morocco than on demonstrations fueled by purely social demands. In general, the Saharan demonstrations take place on fixed anniversaries. They may also be organized in support of a specific prisoner. These are political protest demonstrations, whereas social demonstrations take the form of sit-ins in front of province or municipality gates. As explained, it is a practice used by young jobless graduates; also women who come to demand housing or subsidies as soon as they learn of the administration's intention to distribute some. There are also spontaneous demonstrations by women and children in poor urban neighborhoods when the electricity is turned off, or the public fountain is stopped that they and their families are permitted to use for free.

All these social movements may be explained by the following four massive composite factors: increasing liberalization of political life coupled with the demand for respect of human rights; high unemployment among educated young people; the administration's occasionally heterodox practices, and the effects of a policy based on what now seems an outdated process of elite selection.

Once again, the Sahara is characterized by high unemployment, almost twice as high as in the nation as a whole, despite the fact that unemployment has fallen sharply in recent years.

There is therefore nothing surprising in the fact that young educated jobless persons in the Saharan provinces experience the feelings of deprivation that go with it. Nor is it difficult to explain the high rate of unemployment. The aim here is to identify the relation between that rate and the social movements, which, as mentioned, may also be observed throughout the nation as a whole.

Despite its efforts, the state can no longer meet social demand. The job market is not able to provide positions to new graduates who remain in the Saharan provinces rather than moving to other regions of Morocco. Though during the 1980s and early 1990s the state and the market responded correctly to demand for jobs, this is not been the case since the mid-1990s, a period marked, as we have seen, by a sharp population increase. Certain of the southern provinces experienced record growth: 170% for Oued Ed-Dahab, and as high as 700% for Aousserd.

To these macroeconomic traits must be added other factors, related to the incompetence of the administrative personnel and their unconstructive practices: absenteeism, lack of knowledge about the region, rigidity, inability to predict social demand and events.

The last set of crucial social determinants to be cited in explaining frustration among young Moroccans is the country's "*notable*"-centred policy, practiced with success up to the last decade but no longer relevant to the new social realities of the Saharan provinces.

Local elites—"*notables*"—used to be selected on the basis of their status and ability to mobilize members of their tribe. These elites or their children played a relay role between the state and their tribesmen, in exchange for government-granted advantages, particularly administrative posts and housing subsidies.

This form of government and means of resolving conflicts has shown its limitations. The Morocco of the last two decades is different from what the country was in the 1970s and 80s. In the intensely urbanized southern provinces, *notables* can no longer play the roles they once did. They are faced with increasing resistance from within their own tribes, especially from young people, despite the persistence of clientelist relations.

I have shown in detail how in the late 1980s the school system in Morocco began turning out young, well-educated Sahrawis torn between two worlds, aspiring to the values of modernity discovered as they moved through the university centers while maintaining some ties with members of their tribe. In fact, the young are resisting not only against the tribe itself but also the old ways of selecting local elites. Those elites are generally illiterate and the young see them as backward. Moreover, the experience of increasing economic and social disparities between families within the same tribe is probably more direct and intense for young

Sahrawis than for other young Moroccans. And the political parties, far from being the means of political socialization that the constitution meant them to be, are really no more than vote-securing machines. We see how it is that withdrawal into local identity becomes ineluctable.

In such a situation, characterized by endemic youth unemployment, scarce resources and the lack of any clear vision for the future or definitive solution to the problem of the Sahara, it is easy to imagine how protest develops and why identity-focused strategies seem a winning card for frustrated youth. We can also understand why the mobilizing power of separatist ideas has grown since the late 1990s, especially if we consider that the democratization of political life has actually led to the liberation of a number of what are termed political prisoners, among them Mohamed Daddach, Ali Salem Tamek, Mohamed El Moutawakil, Brahim Noumria, Aminatou Haidar, Houcine Lidri, Larbi Mesaoud, Hmad Hammad and Brahim Dahane.

It also becomes understandable why the most critical individuals are precisely those who received a full education and who have higher chances of social and occupational promotion than earlier and much less educated generations. These people are in general young, and they feel they have been deprived of material and symbolic goods they should have benefited from—a paradox that can be clarified using some of the "theorems" of relative deprivation theory.

Before a brief presentation of the main points of the theory, it is important to outline the social composition of the Saharan population, as it carries with it a set of power relations. By superimposing and combining those two dimensions, we will define the relevant membership and reference groups for this population. Without some notion of these concepts, we cannot hope to understand the protest mechanisms at work. However, membership and reference groups are not determined through sociological analysis of stratification but rather by social representations. In other words, we are only describing the conception that social actors have of reality, not that reality in itself, which may be different from the conception. As W.I Thomas (1929) showed, if we want to understand and explain individuals' actions, it is extremely important to know the meaning they attribute to reality. According to Thomas' theorem, if actors define a situation as real, it *is* real insofar as it causes them to take real actions that then have real consequences. This implies that individuals respond not only to the objective characteristics of a situation but also, and in some cases first and foremost, to the meaning they attribute to that situation.[4]

The first social category is made up of Sahrawis who have been settled in the area for a relatively long time. They continue to enjoy special privileges and above all they maintain close ties with the local authorities; they hold and exercise strong power recognized by the population. This category, which dominates the three other social strata, is itself divided into subgroups, hierarchically ordered in accordance with tribal criteria. It includes a part of the great Rguibat tribe.

The second category is made up of Saharans from other regions of the Sahara, namely Guelmim and Tan Tan. It includes fractions of the Rguibat and other specifically Saharan tribes, particularly the Ait Oussa—meaning it is not made up exclusively of people foreign to the Sahara. This category has a strong urban presence, but its members are in large part dominated by individuals from the first category. Interestingly, the spirit of protest seems strongest in young people from this category. Within this active minority, the most virulently critical individuals are not necessarily Sahrawis but are more likely to be individuals from other Moroccan provinces in search of social recognition, including some who are opinion leaders for the young.

The third social stratum is made up of Sahrawis originally from other Moroccan regions who returned to their region of origin relatively recently, most likely in the early 1990s. They live primarily on state subsidies in uncomfortable neighbourhoods and conditions. They are seen by the other social categories to have undergone a status drop and are without social prestige.

The fourth and last category includes "outsiders" from other regions of Morocco who have immigrated internally in their search for a better job and wage than they could hope to obtain in their home province.

The purpose of this brief presentation is to outline the social framework and hierarchical power relations obtaining among the social categories; also to define the relevant membership groups and groups that these individuals compare their situation with when they undertake collective actions.

In what way can the theory of relative deprivation help us understand the social movements we are concerned with here? It should be recalled that the concepts of relative deprivation and reference groups were first used by Stouffer in his study of the American soldier (1949). The idea is also present in the works of Tocqueville, Durkheim and Weber, and in the thinking of such economists as Duesenberry, Easterlin and Hirschman. The economists stress the importance of the notion of relative versus absolute income: it is crucial to compare to compare two statuses of the same individual at two different moments in time in order to explain paradoxical phenomena that standard economic theory is unable to account for. In this connection it is interesting to note that only very recently, in response to the results of a growing set of economic and sociological studies showing the crucial importance of social networks for correctly understanding how markets work, did the leading theoretician of the Chicago school of economics, Gary Becker, propose changing standard economic theory to integrate this sociological dimension.

One of Stouffer's research results was that privileged groups seemed more inclined than relatively unprivileged ones to criticize the American army promotion system. He observed that military police, members of a corps where promotion was unlikely, said they were satisfied with the promotion system governing their military career, whereas pilots, members of a corps whose members were frequently promoted, were nonetheless—and oddly enough—dissatisfied with the promotion system.

To explain this paradox, Stouffer introduced the notions of relative deprivation and reference group. If at the same age and the same educational and seniority level, the majority of my colleagues are promoted and I am too, I will think that promotion is normal. If on the other hand I am not promoted, I will feel I have been treated unfairly, and will express this feeling by criticizing the occupational mobility system. If, in the group I belong to or the group I refer to when making my assessments, workers are rarely promoted, I will be particularly pleased if I get promoted but I will not have any sense of being unjustly treated if I do not because the majority of my fellow workers will not have been promoted either. The sense of deprivation is felt only in certain conditions.

To take an example of modern economic thinking, Hirschman explains tolerance of inequality in a developing country in terms of the "tunnel effect," a notion directly related to the theory of relative deprivation and reference group. Suppose a driver is driving in a two-lane, one-way tunnel in which traffic has come to a halt. After a certain amount of time during which no cars move in either lane, the driver observes that the cars in the other lane are starting to move forward. The first effect of this is to make him feel better because he thinks the cause of the traffic jam no longer exists and if the other lane is starting to move his will soon be moving too. If he then remains in place for some time while continuing to observe that traffic in the other lane is moving, his expectations or hopes will have been let down. Ultimately, he will get upset and try to correct the apparent injustice by changing lanes, even though his action violates the traffic rule prohibiting drivers to cross the double line between the two lanes. The same is true of inequalities. If my neighbour's or my peer's situation improves, I begin to hope the same will happen to me. If does not, and my hopes are let down, I will feel deprived and try to change the order of things.

In the preceding examples, the reference group and the membership group are the same: I belong to the military police, and when I assess the promotion system I am comparing myself with my fellow policemen. But things do not always work this way. For individuals who have experienced upward (or downward) social mobility, social class of origin is of course not the same as the social class they rise to (or fall from). A given individual in this situation can choose either the class of origin or the class attained as membership or reference group, and any combination permitted by a non-exclusive "or" is possible. This is in fact one reason why researchers find it so difficult to explain their subjects' economic behaviour (e.g., consumption), political behaviour (e.g. voting) and psychosociological behaviour (e.g., feeling of deprivation). The situation of socially mobile persons gave rise to the concept of status inconsistency, developed and systematized by Lenski. We need the notions of membership group, reference group and inconsistency to analyse the contradictions experienced by socially mobile individuals, torn as they seem to be between the expectations of the group they aspire to belong to and those of the group they have moved out of and yet continue to have affective ties to.

If interpreted as a set of rationalist hypotheses, as Boudon proposes (1977), relative deprivation theory is quite useful in understanding political protest in the Sahara and the other regions of Morocco, though it most certainly does not explain them entirely, as I made clear earlier. Testing those hypotheses requires conducting experimental studies of this complex phenomenon, studies that take into account social and power relations as well as the specificity of the Saharan provinces outlined above. However, there is no reason for taking a particularist ethnographic approach, which certainly cannot explain anything given that, as I have stressed, similar phenomena can be observed in other regions of Morocco.[5]

NOTES

1. See among others Davies 1961; Gurr 1968, 1970; Huntington 1968; Drescher 1968; Furet 1971; Skocpol 1979; Cherkaoui 2005.

2. The modernization theories that began to be developed in the late 1950s originate in and are founded on the philosophical conception of modernity developed by the Enlightenment philosophers. The *siècle de la raison* with its optimistic belief in progress provided succeeding generations all the way to our time with apparently inexhaustible matter for reflection. And we are right to think we are the heirs of that tradition. Throughout the nineteenth century, modernity fascinated economists and sociologists, from Comte to Max Weber and Emile Durkheim, from Marx to liberal thinkers such as Schumpeter, who meditated on it constantly and proposed increasingly refined explanatory hypotheses. Evolutionist theories, Marxism, theories on the birth of capitalism, industrial development, and the economy in general, popularized after the Second World War, all derive from this vision, which some readily qualify as western.

   These theories have been the target of a great deal of criticism, much of it sound. They have been attacked as simplistic and powerless to account for the complexity of social change; it has been shown that they were based on fragile empirical data that cannot be used to verify them because of their high level of generality; it has also been maintained that theories of convergence and democratic transition are nothing but sweetened versions of development-stage theory. The critiques led theorists to develop local, conditional models, limited to carefully circumscribed areas.

3. On Morocco's falling fertility rate see studies by the Centre d'Etudes et de Recherches Démographiques of the Haut Commissariat du Plan; also Courbage 2006 and Courbage and Todd 2006.

4. See Merton's "self-fulfilling prophecy" theory (1968).

5. See my synthesis of the theory of relative deprivation (Cherkaoui 2002).

Conclusion

To suggest a conclusion to this study would mean that the intellectual project stops at this point. But my research does not end here. I am well aware that some ideas and conjectures may be worthy of closer attention and ought to be challenged by new data. The people whose actions and ultimate ends I am trying to understand will most likely continue both their interrupted dialogue, and their age-old conflict. But that should not stop us from touching briefly on the main issues raised in this sociological study. The first deals with the geopolitical issues that confront the Sahara. The second is the nature of the social bonds that tie the Sahrawi peoples to the Sunni Muslim and Berber-Arab space that is known as Morocco.

I have initially tried to show how the Algerian leadership have made the Sahara into one of the central issues around which their foreign policy has revolved since independence. It has not been difficult to show the continual contradictions between their rhetoric during the first years of Algerian independence and their behaviour in relation to their neighbours. But even if one were to lose all faith in their promises, so often proclaimed but never kept, it remains true that some will continue to be impressed by the cries of indignation with which they fill the meetings of international organisations for the defence of principles with which they have no truck. Is it necessary to recall that they had no hesitation in violating these principles when France asked them to consult the Tuaregs? Should we add that the peoples of the vast Eastern Sahara which was an integral part of the Kingdom of Morocco until the beginning of the 20th century, and later annexed by force of arms by French Algeria, have not yet had the right to speak?

Furthermore it has been simple to show that the problem of the Sahara cannot be understood if the territorial dispute between Algeria and Morocco is not considered, as well as what I have called the imperial *hubris* of the masters of Algiers. I suggest an explanation of this that runs counter to the rather media-friendly theory of Hardt and Negri which argues for the end of the sovereignty of the nation-state and the emergence of a sole global power. Their thesis takes little account of the creation of great regional powers. Look at Iran, for instance. By exploiting the interpretational errors of American strategists the Iranians have been able, in a matter of years, to come close to realising a dream they have nourished for many centuries. Besides the common interests of the Moscow-Teheran-Algiers axis, the Algerian stratocracy now perceive the Iranian leadership as their gurus. They will be greatly encouraged by the unexpected success of their mentors. They will achieve their objective if Morocco loses its last Saharan provinces. The oldest state in Africa apart from Egypt will be condemned henceforth to play second fiddle in a region that it has largely fashioned from the end of the 8th century. Its southern borders will be under constant threat , because a vassal state in Western Sahara will brought into being by the masters of Algiers.

In addition to the tensions and the non-cooperative games between Algeria and Morocco whose underlying theoretical models I have attempted to decode, this study is also concerned with the problems that the risk of balkanization poses for a region stretching from the Atlantic to the Red Sea

Moreover this sociological analysis is designed to place the problems posed by the notion of the autonomy of the Saharan regions within the context of the vast programme of reform that Morocco has pursued for more than a decade, and described as a *"friedliche Revolution"*, by *Der Spiegel*. Its choice of the difficult route towards federal democracy is an alternative to the stratocracy that appears to fascinate the other states of the region

The second main thread of this study has been to examine a central issue for the region, that of the social integration of the Sahrawi peoples. I have said that without the Sahara the history of Morocco cannot be understood, and without Morocco, the Sahara is no more than a desert. The sentence might seem too emphatic, but it expresses what the historians and anthropologists of the region have clearly demonstrated.

In order to evaluate this proposition I have used all of the available demographic, economic and sociological data of the last four decades, and deployed the most refined statistical and mathematical models, with the aim of testing the hypothesis of a relatively good integration of these peoples. The conclusions of this study all lead in the same direction, that of the emergence and strengthening of a dense network of social and economic bonds that integrated the Saharan provinces and helped them to leave the state of destitution in which they found themselves during colonisation, and allowed them to modernise due to an effective policy of affirmative action. One pertinent example is that of school enrolment: the rate of enrolment of the young Sahrawi generations is now higher than that of their peers in the most affluent and socially endowed Moroccan regions. The importance of such a result can be appreciated by the fact that at the end of Spanish colonisation in 1975, there were only 2300 children enrolled in primary schools and not a single secondary school.

For theoretical and practical reasons that I discuss in the first chapter of the second part of this book, I have also conducted a survey which offers what is, in my view, the best indicator of social integration: what I term matrimonial exchange. To this end I have perused all the *Adoulien* registers which record the marriage contracts for the years 1960 to 2006 in order to test the hypothesis that in the Sahara, where endogamy is the rule, heterogamous marriage between Sahrawis and the rest of the Moroccan has gradually increased. The survey covers about 30,000 marriage certificates. It is the only survey of its type. The data it makes available has enabled me to test all types of regional homogamy and endogamy. I will admit that the results of this analysis were unpredictable, surprising even. I will merely cite one as an example. In forty years the rate of endogamy went from more 97% to less than 55%. Almost all the heterogeneous marriages were between Sahrawis and Moroccans from other regions. I would add that this result would have been even more impressive if I had had available the marriage contracts of Sahrawis who lived in other regions of Morocco than the Sahara. In this population, it is most likely that heterogamous marriage rate reaches record levels.

To attempt to divide families between two political entities would thus be socially, politically and morally prejudicial from the point of view of their human rights and their clear desire to live together. The dilemma this would pose to those placed in the role of a god-like decision maker, would be worse than that experienced by Lord Mountbatten and Cyril Radcliffe at the time of the partition of British India into two independent nations. I would wager that this supreme judge would have to consider the case of East Timor before pronouncing his sentence.

I have not forgotten those social and political movements of the Sahara and within the whole of Morocco that have been the consequence of rapid modernization, nor the multiple dimensions of the integration process, nor in particular the great liberalization of political life. These were, in my view, entirely predictable. Tocqueville would have both forecast and explained them. But in the chapter devoted to this subject, I have not suggested that my conclusions are anything other than provisional.

I cannot, in the end, write the last words of this study without thinking in particular about the Maghrebin people who have become powerless witnesses to a form of artificial and exhausting dissension. It would be wrong to believe that they are more worried about their daily bread than concerned with the issues about their union. To think so would be an insult to their intelligence.

Appendix of Maps

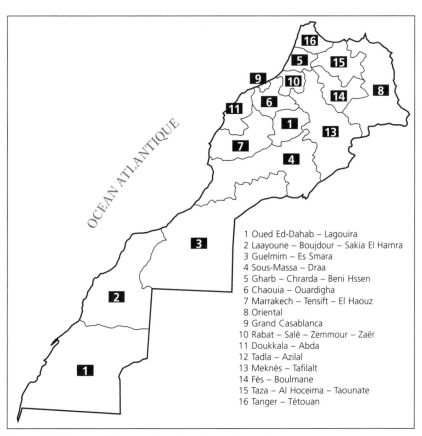

1 Oued Ed-Dahab – Lagouira
2 Laayoune – Boujdour – Sakia El Hamra
3 Guelmim – Es Smara
4 Sous-Massa – Draa
5 Gharb – Chrarda – Beni Hssen
6 Chaouia – Ouardigha
7 Marrakech – Tensift – El Haouz
8 Oriental
9 Grand Casablanca
10 Rabat – Salé – Zemmour – Zaër
11 Doukkala – Abda
12 Tadla – Azilal
13 Meknès – Tafilalt
14 Fès – Boulmane
15 Taza – Al Hoceima – Taounate
16 Tanger – Tétouan

Map A3: *Map of Morocco's administrative regions*

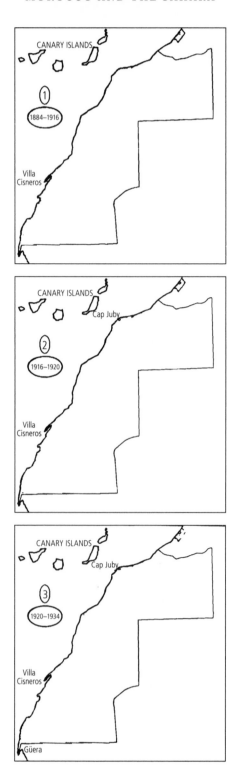

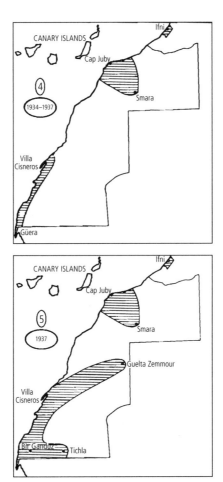

Map A2: *The different phases of the partial Spanish occupation of Western Sahara, 1884–1937*

Source: *Le Sahara Occidental devant la Cour Internationale de Justice. Mémoire présenté par le Royaume du Maroc*, p. 25

Map A3 (Overleaf): *Map of the Moroccan Empire 1843 or 1845?*

Source: *Exploration scientifique de l'Algérie pendant les années 1840, 1841, 1842.* Paris, Imprimerie Royale, 1846.

Maps A4 to A9 (pages 186–188): *French colonial expansion in the Sahara and the incoporation of Moroccan regions into French Algeria*

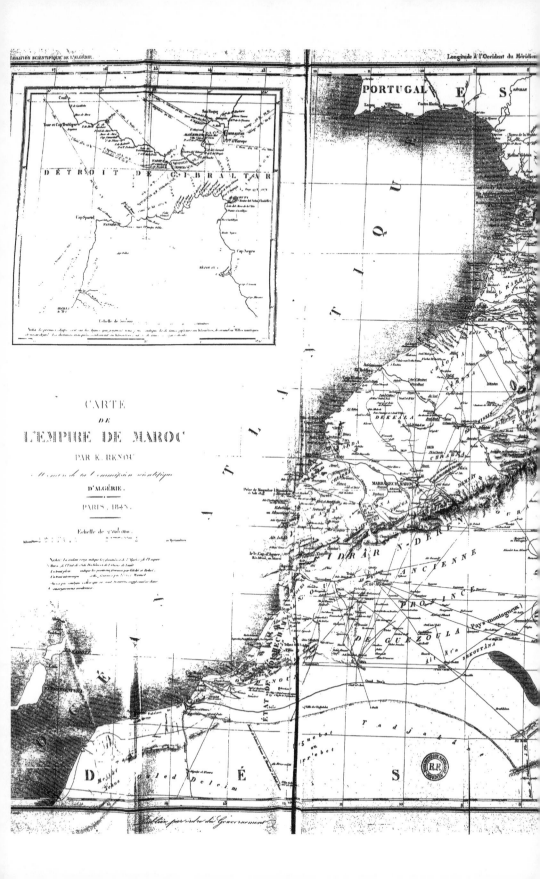

PORTUGAL ES

DÉTROIT DE GIBRALTAR

Cap Spartel

Cap Negro

Échelle de ...

CARTE
DE
L'EMPIRE DE MAROC
PAR E. RENOU
Attaché de la Commission scientifique
D'ALGÉRIE.
PARIS, 1848.

Échelle de 2.000.000

DEKKALA

MARRAKECH MAROC

IDRAR-N-DERN-OU-ATLAS ANCIENNE

PROVINCE

DE GUEZOULA Pays montagneux

Tadjakant

D É S

Publiée par ordre du Gouvernement

R.20

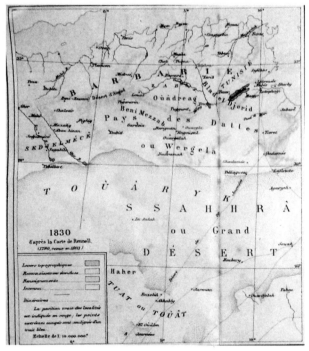

Map A4: *1830*

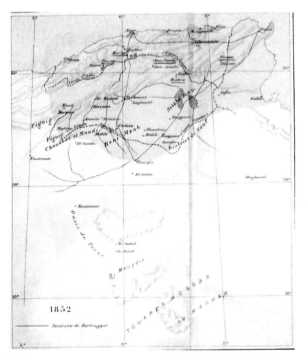

Map A5: *1852*

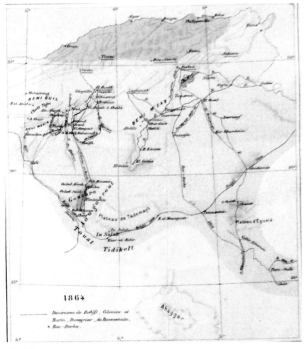

Map A6: *1864*

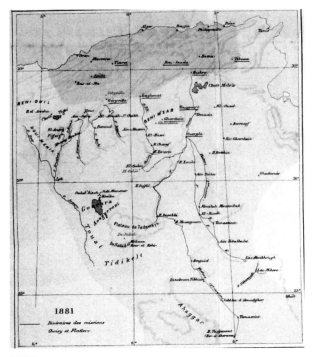

Map A7: *1881*

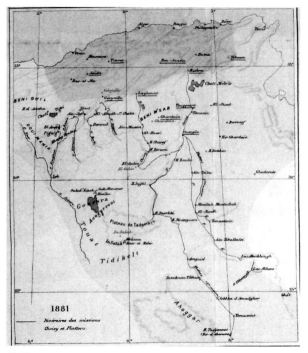

Map A7: *1881*

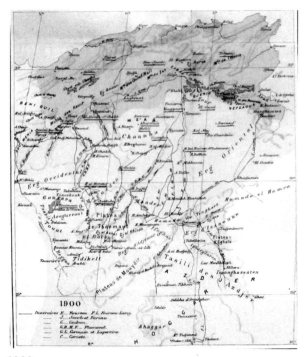

Map A8: *1900*

Bibliography

Aboumalek, M. (1994) *Qui épouse qui? Le mariage en milieu urbain*, Casablanca, Edition Afrique Orient.

Addi, L. (1990) *L'impasse du populisme. L'Algérie, collectivité politique et État en construction*, Alger, E.N.A.L.

Ammour, K., C. *et al.* (1974) *La Voie algérienne. Les contradictions d'un développement national*, Paris, Maspero.

Amsden, R. (1968) *Foreign Policy and Its Role in Nation-Building in Algeria*, Ann Arbor.

Aron, R. (1959) *La société industrielle et la guerre*, Paris, Plon.

——— (1962) *Paix et guerre entre les nations*, Paris, Calman-Lévy.

Axelrod, R. (1984) *The Evolution of Cooperation*, New York, Basic Books.

Baechler, J. (2006) *Esquisse d'une histoire universelle*, Paris, Fayard.

Balta, P. & Rulleau, C. (1981) *L'Algérie des Algériens. Vingt ans après*, Paris, Les éditions ouvrières.

Becker, G. (1968). "Crime and Punishment: An Economic Approach", *The Journal of Political Economy*, 76: 169–217.

Benoist, J.R. de (1979) *La Balkanisation de l'Afrique Occidentale Française*, Dakar, Nouvelles éditions africaines.

Bergman, W.K. (1981) *Arms for Morocco: The Western Sahara Conflict.* American African Affairs Association.

Berlin, I. (1973) *Trois essais sur la condition juive*, Paris, Pocket.

Berramdane, A. (1987) *Le Maroc et l'Occident (1800–1974)*, Paris, Karthala.

——— (1992) *Le Sahara Occidental: enjeu maghrébin*, Paris, Karthala.

Birnbaum, P. (1997 ed.) *Sociologie des nationalismes*, Paris, Presses Universitaires de France.

Blalock, A.B. (1968 ed.) *Methodology in Social Research*, New York, McGraw Hill Book Co.

Blau, P. (1964) *Exchange and Power in Social Life*, New York, Wiley.

—— (1977) *Inequality and Heterogeneity. A Primitive Theory of Social Structure*, New York, Free Press.

Blau, P. & Schwartz, J. (1984) *Crosscutting Social Circles: Testing a Macrostructural Theory of Intergroup Relations*, New York, Academic Press.

Blin, L. (1990) *L'Algérie, du Sahara au Sahel*, Paris, L'Harmattan.

Boudon, R. (1973a) *L'inégalité des chances*, Paris, A. Colin.

—— (1973b) *Mathematical Structures of Social Mobility*, Amsterdam, Elsevier.

—— (1977) *Effets pervers et ordre social*, Paris, Presses Universitaires de France.

—— (1979) *La logique du social*, Paris, Hachette.

—— (1998) "Social Mechanisms Without Black Boxes", in Hedström and Swedberg (1998 eds).

—— (2003) *Raison, bonnes raisons*, Paris, Presses Universitaires de France.

—— (2004) *The Poverty of Relativism*, Oxford, Bardwell Press.

Bozon, M. & Héran, F. (1988) "La découverte du conjoint", *Population*, 43rd year, no. 1, Jan–Feb 1988: 121–50.

Brahimi, B. (1990) *Le Pouvoir, la presse et les intellectuels en Algérie*, Paris, L'Harmattan.

Briggs, L.C. (1960) *Tribes of the Sahara Desert*, Cambridge, Harvard University Press.

Brower, A. (1984) *Marxist Theories of Imperialism: A Critical Survey*, London, Routledge and Kegan Paul.

Brubaker, R. & F. Cooper, F. (2000) "Beyond 'identity'", *Theory and Society*, 29, 1: 1–47.

Brubaker, R., Loveman, M. & Stamatov, P. (2004) "Ethnicity as cognition", *Theory and Society*, 33, 1: 31–64.

Cain, P. (2002) *Hobson and Imperialism: Radicalism, New Liberalism, and Finance*, New York, Oxford University Press.

Caratini, S. (1985) *Le territoire des Rgaybat (1610–1934)*, Paris, L'Harmattan.

—— (1989) "A propos du mariage 'arabe'. Discours endogame et pratiques exogames: l'exemple des Rgaybat du nord-ouest saharien", *L'homme*, 29, 110: 30–49.

—— (1995) "Du modèle aux pratiques: ambivalence de la filiation et de l'alliance chez les Rgaybat de l'ouest-saharien", *L'homme*, 35, 133: 33–50.

Chazel, F. Boudon, R., Lazarsfeld, P. (1970 eds) *L'analyse des processus sociaux*, Paris, La Haye, Mouton.

Cherkaoui, M. (1982) *Les changements du système éducatif en France, 1950–1980*, Paris, Presses Universitaires de France.

—— (1998) *Naissance d'une science sociale*, Geneva, Paris, Droz.

—— (2005) *Invisible Codes. Essays on Generative Mechanisms*, Oxford, Bardwell Press.

—— (2006) *Le paradoxe des conséquences. Essai sur une théorie wébérienne des effets inattendus et non voulus des actions*, Geneva, Paris, Droz.

—— (2007) *Good Intentions. Max Weber and the Paradox of Unintended Consequences*, Oxford, Bardwell Press, translation of Cherkaoui (2006).

Chelhod, J. (1965) "Le mariage avec la cousine parallèle dans le système arabe", *L'homme*, 5, 3–4: 113–73.

Coleman, J.S. (1968) "The Mathematical Study of Change" in Blalock (1968 ed).

—— (1990) *Foundations of Social Theory*, Cambridge, Belknap Press of Harvard University Press.

Coleman, J.S. Katz, E. Mentzel, (1957)"The Diffusion of an Innovation Among Physicians", Fr. tr. in Chazel, Boudon, Lazarsfeld (1970 eds).

Collier, P. (2000) "Rebellion as a Quasi-Criminal Activity", *Journal of Conflict Resolution*, 44, 6 : 839–53.

Connor, W. (1994) *Ethnonationalism. The Quest for Understanding*, Princeton, Princeton University Press.

Coser, L. (1956) *The Functions of Social Conflict*, The Free Press of Glencoe.

Cour Internationale de Justice (1979–82) *Sahara Occidental*, 5 volumes, The Hague.

Courbage, Y. (2006) "L'accélération de la transition: un bonus démographique pour le Maroc", in Haut Commissariat au Plan (2006).

Courbage, Y. & Todd, E. (2006) *Révolution culturelle au Maroc: le sens d'une transition démographique*, Communications et Institutions.

Coustillière, J.F. (2005a) "Méditerranée: 5 + 5 et initiative de sécurité" *Revue de Défense Nationale*, no. 5.

—— (2005b) "Enjeux de l'initiative française de sécurité en format 5 + 5", *Les Cahiers de Mars*, no. 185.

—— (2006) "Questions de sécurité et de défense en Méditerranée: les différentes initiatives multinationales de coopération et de partenariat proposées", *Revue des Etudes Internationales de l'AEI* à Tunis, no. 3.

Damis, J. (1983) *Conflict in Northwest Africa. The Western Sahara Dispute*, Stanford, Hoover Institutions Press.

—— (1962) "Toward a Theory of Revolution", *American Sociological Review*, 6, 1: 5–19.

Dessens, P. (1978) *La question du Sahara Occidental*, Alger, Ministère des Affaires Etrangères.

Deutsch, K. (1969) *Nationalism and Social Communication*, Cambridge, Mass., The MIT Press.

Drescher, S. (1968) *Dilemmas of Democracy. Tocqueville and Modernization*, Pittsburgh, University of Pittsburgh Press.

Durkheim, E. (1895) *De la division du travail social*, Paris, Presses Universitaires de France, nouvelle éd.

—— (1897) *Le suicide*, Paris, Presses Universitaires de France, nouvelle éd.

—— (1900) "La sociologie en France au XIXè siècle", *Revue Bleue*, XIII: 609–613 & 647–652 reprinted in Durkheim (1970)

—— (1912) *Les formes élémentaires de la vie religieuse*, Paris, Presses Universitaires de France, new edn.

—— (1970) *La science sociale et l'action*, textes réunis par Filloux, Paris, Presses Universitaires de France.

Ehrlich, I., *et al.* (2006 eds) *The Economics of Crime*, Cheltenham, Edward Elgar Publishing.

El Houdaïgui, R. (2003) *La politique étrangère sous le règne de Hassan II. Acteurs, enjeux et processus décisionnels*, Paris, L'Harmattan.

Etienne, B. (1977) *L'Algérie, cultures et révolution*, Paris, Le Seuil.

Gallisot, R. (1988) *Maghreb-Algérie, classes et nation*, Arcantère, Paris.

Gellner, E. (1969) *Saints of the Atlas*, London, Weidenfeld & Nicolson.

—— (1983) *Nations and Nationalism*, Oxford, Basil Blackwell.

—— (1999) "La religion et le profane. Islam, nationalisme et marxisme au XXè siècle", *Commentaire*, 85: 107–113.

Girard, A. (1964) *Le choix du conjoint*, Paris, Presses Universitaires de France.

Griliches, Z. (1957) "Hybrid Corn: An Exploration in the Economics of Technological Change", *Econometrica*, XXV, 501–522.

Grimaud, N. (1984) *La Politique extérieure de l'Algérie*, Paris, Karthala.

Gurr, T. (1971) *When Men Revolt and Why*, New York, The Free Press.

Hammoudi, A. (1974) "Segmentarité, stratification sociale, pouvoir politique et sainteté. Réflexions sur les thèses de Gellner", *Hesperis Tamuda*, 15: 147–180.

—— (1980) "Sainteté, pouvoir et société: Tamagrout aux XVIIè et XVIIIè siècles", *Annales*, 35, 3–4: 615–41.

Hardt, M. & Negri, A. (2000) *Empire*, Cambridge, Harvard University Press.

Harsany, J. (1968) "Individualistic and Functionalistic Explanations in the Light of Game Theory: The Example of Social Status", in Lakatos and Musgrave (1968 eds).

Haut Commissariat au Plan (2004) *Carte de la pauvreté communale*, Rabat, imprimerie El Maarif Al Jadida.

—— (2004) *Pauvreté, développement humain et social au Maroc*, Rabat, imprimerie El Maarif Al Jadida.

Hedström, P. (2005) *Dissecting the Social. On the Principles of Analytical Sociology*, Cambridge, Cambridge University Press.

Hedström, P. & Swedberg, R. (1998) *Social Mechanisms. An Analytical Approach to Social Theory*, Cambridge, Cambridge University Press.

Hésiode, *Les travaux et les jours*, Paris, Les Belles Lettres.

Hirschman, A.O. (1977) *The Passions and the Interests. Political Arguments for Capitalism Before Its Triumph*, Princeton, Princeton University Press.

Hobson, J.A. (1902) *Imperialism*, London, Allen and Unwin.

Homans, G. (1961) *Social Behavior: Its Elementary Forms*, New York, Harcourt Brace.

Huntington, S. (1957) *The Soldier and the State. The Theory and Politics of Civil-Military Relations*, Belknap Press, 2005.

—— (1968) *Political Order in Changing Societies*, New Haven, Yale University Press.

Ibn Khaldun (1377) *Prolégomènes au Discours sur l'histoire universelle*, Fr. tr. Beirut, Presses de l'Imprimerie Catholique.

Institut des hautes études marocaines (1930) *Etudes, notes et documents sur le Sahara Occidental*, Rabat, Paris, Librairie E. Larose.

International Crisis Group (2005) "Islamist Terrorism in the Sahel: Fact or Fiction?", *Africa Report* no. 92.

Janowitz, M. (1960) *The Professional Soldier. A Social and Political Portrait*, New York, The Free Press.

—— (1962) *The Military in the Political Development of New Nations. An Essay in Comparative Analysis*, Chicago, Chicago University Press.

Julien, Ch. A. (1978) *Le Maroc face aux impérialismes*, Paris, Editions Jeune Afrique.

Kant, E. (1795) *Zum ewigen Frieden. Ein philosophischer Entwurf*, in *Kant's gesammelte Schriften*, Berlin, Reimer & de Gruyter, Fr. tr. *Projet de paix perpétuelle*, Paris, Vrin, 1975.

Krueger, A. B. & Maleckova, J. (2003) "Education, Poverty and Terrorism: Is There a Causal Connection?", *Journal of Economic Perspectives*, 17, 4: 119–44.

Labat, R. (1970) *Les religions du Proche-Orient asiatique. Textes babyloniens, ougaritiques, hittites*, Paris, Fayard.

Lakatos, I. & Musgrave, A. (1968 eds) *Problems in the Philosophy of Science*, Amsterdam, North-Holland Publishing Co.

Lamchichi, A. (1991) *L'Algérie en crise*, L'Harmattan, Paris.

Laroui, A. (2005) *Le Maroc et Hassan II. Un témoignage*, Rabat, Presses Inter Universitaires & Centre Culturel Arabe.

Lasswell, H. (1997) *Essays on the Garrison State*, New Brunswick, Transaction.

Leca, J. & Katin, J.-C. (1975) *L'Algérie politique. Institutions et régime*, Paris, Presses de la Fondation Nationale des Sciences Politiques.

Leveau, R. (1993) *Le Sabre et le turban. L'avenir du Maghreb*, Paris, F. Bourin.

Lockwood, D. (1964) "Social Integration and System Integration", in Zollschan and Hirsch (1964 eds), pp. 244–57.

Maazouzi, M. (1976) *L'Algérie et les étapes successives de l'amputation du territoire marocain*, Casablanca, Dar El Kitab.

—— (1976) *Tindouf et les frontières méridionales du Maroc*, Casablanca, Dar El Kitab.

—— (2004) *Un demi-siècle pour l'intégrité territoriale*, Rabat, Imprimerie El Maarif Al Jadida.

Mann, M. (2003) *Incoherent Empire*, London, Verso.

Marchat, H. (1960) *La question des frontières terrestres du Maroc*, Paris, La documentation française.

Martel, A. (1965) *Les confins saharo-tripolitains de la Tunisie (1881–1911)*, Paris, Presses Universitaires de France.

Martin, A.G.P (1923) *Quatre siècles d'histoire marocaine*, Paris, Félix Alcan.

Martinoli, E. (1998) *L'Ouest saharien, état des lieux et matériaux de recherche*, Paris, L'Harmattan.

Mawerdi (+1058) *Les statuts gouvernementaux*, Fr. tr. Fagan, Paris, Le Sycomore.

Merton, R.K. (1968) *Social Theory and Social Structure*, New York, The Free Press.

Miège, L. (1962) *Le Maroc et l'Europe*, Paris, Presses Universitaires de France.

Mills, C.W. (1959) *The Power Elite*, New York, Oxford University Press.

Mohsen-Fenan, K. (2002 ed) *L'Algérie: une improbable sortie de crise*, Paris, Institut français des relations internationales.

—— (1997) *Sahara occidental. Les enjeux d'un conflit régional*, Paris, editions du CNRS.

Mommsen, W. (1981) *Theories of Imperialism*, London, Weidenfield and Nicholson.

Montagne, R. (1930) *Les Berbères et le Makhzen au sud du Maroc*, Paris, Félix Alcan.

Montesquieu, C. de (1748) *L'esprit des lois*, in *Œuvres Complètes*, Paris, Gallimard, Edition de la Pléiade.

Nadel, S.F. (1970) *The Theory of Social Structure*, London, Cohen & West.

Naimi, M. (2004) *La dynamique des alliances ouest-sahariennes. De l'espace géographique à l'espace social*, Paris, Editions de la Maison des Sciences de l'Homme.

O'Donnell, G., Schmitter, P., and Whitehead, L. (1986 eds) *Transition from Authoritarian Rule*, Baltimore, Johns Hopkins University Press.

Owen, R. & Sutcliffe, B. (1981 eds) *Studies in the Theory of Imperialism*, Harlow, Longman.

Parsons, T. (1951) *The Social System*, New York, Free Press.

Rapoport, A. (1960) *Fights, Games and Debates*, Ann Arbor, University of Michigan Press.

Rapoport, A. *et al.* (1965) *Prisonner's Dilemma: A Study in Conflict and Cooperation*, Ann Arbor, The University of Michigan Press.

Renan, E. (1882) *Qu'est-ce qu'une nation*, in *Œuvres complètes*, Paris, Calman-Lévy.

Rezette, R. (1975) *Le Sahara Occidental et les frontières marocaines*, Paris, Nel.

Romilly, J.de (1947) *Thucydide et l'impérialisme athénien. La pensée de l'historien et la genèse de l'œuvre*, Paris, Les Belles Lettres.

Rosen, S. (1973 ed) *Testing the Theories of the Miliary-Industrial Complex*, Lexington, Lexington Books.

Rouquié, A. (1982) *L'Etat militaire en Amérique latine*, Paris, Le Seuil.

Schumpeter, J. (1951) *Imperialism and Social Classes*, New York, Augustus M. Kelley.

Schelling, T. (1978) *Micromotives and Macrobehavior*, New York, Norton & Co.

Shils, E. (1995) "Nation, Nationalism and Civil Society", in *Nations and Nationalism*, 1(1): 93–118.

Simmel, G. (1908) *Soziologie. Untersuchungen über die Formen der Vergesellschaftung*, Berlin, Duncker & Humblot.

Slater, J. & Nardi, T. (1972) *The Military-Industrial Complex. A Reassessment*, Beverly Hills, Sage Publications.

Smith, A. (1992) "Chosen Peoples: Why Ethnic Groups survive?", *Ethnic and Racial Studies*, 15 : 440–53.

Snyder, G.H. (1971) "Prisoner's Dilemma and 'Chicken' Models in International Politics", *International Studies Quarterly*, 15: 66–103.

Stora, B. (1995) *L'Algérie en 1995: la guerre, l'histoire, la politique*, Paris, Michalon.

Tarde, G. (1890) *Les lois de l'imitation*, Paris, Félix Alcan, nouvelle édition, Paris, Geneva, Slatkine, 1979.

Thomas, W.I. & Thomas, D. (1929) *The Child in America*, 2nd ed., New York, Alfred A. Knopf.

Thucydides (1953–1972), *La guerre du Péloponnèse*, Fr. tr. Jacqueline de Romilly, Paris, Les belles lettres.

Tocqueville, A. de (1856) *L'Ancien Régime et la Révolution*, édition des *Œuvres complètes,* Paris, Gallimard.

Trout, E.F. (1969) *Morroco's Saharan Frontiers*, Geneva, Droz.

Villiers, G. de (1987) *L'État-démiurge: le cas algérien*, Paris, L'Harmattan.

Weber, M. (1895) *Die Nationalstaat und die Volkswirtschaftspolitik,* in Weber (1921).

—— (1918) *Parlament und Regierung im neugeordneten Deutschland,* in Weber (1921).

—— (1917) *Wahlrecht und Demokratie in Deutschland,* in Weber (1921).

—— (1921) *Gesammelte politische Schriften,* Tübingen, Mohr.

—— (1922) *Wirtschaft und Gesellschaft,* Tübingen, Mohr.

Yefsah, A. (1982) *Le Processus de légitimation du pouvoir militaire et la construction de l'État en Algérie,* Paris, Anthropos.

Zollschan, G. & Hirsch, W. (1964 eds) *Explorations in Social Change,* London, Routledge and Kegan Paul.

Index

Abbasids, 19
Abdesslam, Belaïd, 17
Aboumalek, Mostafa, 157
Addi, Lahouari, 37
Adoul, 77, 141, 157
Adrar Et-Tmart, 59
Adrar Souttouf, 59
Afghanistan, 41, 42
Africa x, 3, 13, 18, 42, 45, 47, 48, 60
Ahl Barakallahn, 58
Ahl Ma Al Ainain, 58
Ain Oussara, 10
Ain-Salah, 1
Ait Lahcen, 58
Ait Mousa Ou Ali, 58
Ait Ousa, 58
Al Qaida, 41, 45
Alaoui, 3
Alexandria (Summit), 14
Algeria x, xii, 2, 10–28, 30–32, 35, 36, 42,
    44–46, 54, 56, 57, 63, 65, 66, 77
Algerian National Revolutionary
    Council, 15
Ali Salem Tamek, 172
Almohad, 3
Almoravid, 3
Al-Para, Abderrazak, 41
Amgala (battles of), 17

Ammouni, Fouad, 59
Ammour, Kader, 37
Amnesty International, 63, 65
Amsden, Robert Mortimer, 37
Annan, Kofi, 55
Aousserd, 124, 125, 127, 129, 161, 162–
    164, 166, 167, 171
Argentina, 11
Aron, Raymond, 18, 27, 37, 44
Aroussiyin, 58
Assa-Zag, 124, 127
Atlantic, 2, 4, 28, 41, 57, 60
Atlas, 56, 149
Axelrod, Robert, 35, 79

Baechler, Jean, 37
Bai'a, 59
Baker, James, 59
Balta, Paul, 37
Becker, Gary, 46, 174
Belarus, 11
Belkhadem, Abdelaziz, 30
Belkheir, Larbi, 21
Ben Ali, 29
Ben Bella, Ahmed, 14, 34
Benoist, J.R. de, 47
Berlin, Isaïah, 70, 79
Berque, Jacques, 80

Bir Aioun, 14
Bir Romane, 14
Blau ,Peter, 79, 149
Blin, Louis, 37
Boudiaf, Mohamed, 21
Boudon, Raymond, 36, 48, 50, 118, 145, 175
Boujdour, 84, 102, 103, 110, 116, 117, 124, 127, 133, 134, 161, 163, 164, 166, 167
Boumediene, Houari, 14, 16, 17, 21, 22, 34
Bourguiba, Habib, 14
Bouteflika, Abdelaziz, 21, 22
Bozon, Michel, 157
Brahimi, Brahim, 37
Brazil, 11
Brecht, Bertolt, 26
Briggs, Lloyd Cabot, 65
Brower, Anthony, 36
Brubaker, Rogers, 50

Cain, Paul, 36
Canary Islands, 60, 182, 183
Caratini, Sophie, 157
Casablanca, 41, 53, 74, 79, 82, 84, 85, 109, 110, 124, 125, 127, 128, 133, 140, 141, 143, 152
Castro, Fidel, 19
Cato, 12
Centre d'études et de recherches démographiques Ddu Haut Commissariat au Plan, 176
Chad, 28, 41, 42, 57
Chadli Bendjedid, 21, 22
Chelhod, Joseph, 138
Chemkhani, Ali, 11
Chenagra, 58
Cherkaoui, Mohamed xi, 50, 79, 118, 176
Chichaoua, 84, 85, 125, 126, 128
China, 10, 11, 19
Chorfa, 1, 58
Clinton, William Jefferson (Bill), 40
Coffinhal, Pierre-André, 5
Coleman, James S., 50, 79, 118
Colonieu, Victor, 59
Comte, Auguste, 27, 30, 37, 176
Connor, Walter, 78
Coser, Lewis, 79
Courbage, Youssef, 176
Cramer (V De), 147

Daddach, Mohamed, 172
Dahane, Brahim, 172
Damis, John, 37
Davies, James, 50, 176
Dessens, Pierre, 37
Deutsch, Karl, 78
Draa, 58, 59, 76, 110
Drescher, Seymour, 176
Duesenberry, James Stemble, 173
Durkheim, Emile, 37, 74, 79, 140, 173, 176

Easterlin, Richard A., 173
Egypt, 11, 12, 29, 178
Ehrlich, Isaac, 46
Eickelman, Dale F., 80
Eisenhower, Dwight David, 17
Eizenstat, Stuart, 40
El Moutawakil, Mohamed, 172
Empire (Soviet), 35, 48; (Ottoman), 13; (British), 18; (Arab Muslim), 19; (Habsburg), 19; (Chinese, Indian, Greek, Roman, Byzantine and Arabo-Muslim), 31; (Moroccan), 183
Enkidu, 36
Es Salam, 10
Escarna, 58
Essaouira, 58, 126
Es-Smara, 84, 110, 124, 125, 127, 133, 134, 161, 163, 164, 166, 167
Etienne, Bruno, 37
Europe, 5, 12, 23, 40–44, 48, 54, 59
Evian, 28

Facts on International Relations and Security Trends, 63
Ferguson, Adam, 37
Ferhat, Abbas, 14
Fès, 110, 125, 127, 133, 134, 141, 181
Figuig, 84, 85, 125, 126, 128
Filala, 58
Fisher (indices), 86
Fondo Documental del Instituto Nacional Estadistico, 78
Fort Saint Louis, 14
Fouikat, 58
France x, 2, 11, 13, 15, 17, 43, 47, 49, 62, 63, 65, 74, 160, 177
Furet, François, 176

Gaïd Salah, Ahmed, 11
Gallisot, René, 37
Gara, Djelibet, 16
Gellner, Ernest, 40, 69, 79, 80
Germany (Federal), 55
Ghana, 42
Giap Vo Nguyen, 19
Gilgamesh, 36
Girard, Alain, 157
Global Rights, 53
Global War on Terror, 42
Goldstein (theory of Joshua), 14
Gourara, 15
Greece, 19
Griliches, Zvi, 118
Grimaud, Nicole, 37
Guelmim, 127, 142, 173
Guelmim-Es-Smara, 84, 110, 124, 125, 133, 134
Guenaïza, Abdelmalek, 11
Guevara, Ernesto Rafael (Che Guevara), 19
Gulf, 12, 29, 30
Gulf Cooperation Council, 12
Gurr, Ted, 50, 176

Haidar, Aminatou, 172
Hammad, Hmad, 172
Hammoudi, Abdellah, 80
Haouz, 58, 110, 125, 126, 181
Hardt, Michael, 36, 80, 178
Harsany, John, 79
Hassan II, 14, 16, 34, 35, 55
Hedström, Peter, 118
Héran, François, 157
Hesiod, 13, 36
High Commission for Planning, 54, 77, 123, 124, 128, 130, 131, 132, 133, 134
High Government Committee, 21
Hirschman, Albert Otto, 37, 173, 174
Hobbes, Thomas, 48, 79
Hobson, John Atkinson, 18
Homans, George C., 79
Hume, David, 40, 79
Huntington, Samuel, 23, 37, 176
Hussein, Saddam, 20
Husson, Michel, 37

Ibn, Khaldun, 60
Ifni, 3, 76, 142, 183

Ifrane, 16, 126
Ihamed, 1
Imraguen, 57, 58
India, 11, 12, 180
Indus, 41
Inshiri, 58
Institut des hautes études marocaines, 65
Institute of Higher Education of Shanghai Jiao Tong University, 5
International Atomic Energy Agency, 11
International Court of Justice, 2, 28, 59
International Crisis Group, 45, 49
International Monetary Fund, 77
International Relations and Security Network, 63
Iran, 11–13, 29, 178
Iraq, 20, 29, 30, 42
Islamic Salvation Front, 30
Israel, 11
Italy, 43
Izerguiin, 58

Jakana, 58
Janowitz, Morris, 37
Jbel Bani, 58
Jing, Zhiyuan, 11
Joint Organization of Saharan Regions, 14
Joint Task Force Aztec Silence, 42
Jordan, 29

Kabyle, 30
Kadhafi, Mouammar, 16
Kalfi Ali, 21
Kant, Emmanuel, 27
Katin, J.-C., 37
Katz, Elihu, 118
Khatami, Mohammad, 11
Koran, 141
Ksour, 58
Kurd, 30

Laaroussian, 58
Laayoune, 84, 110, 115, 116, 117, 124, 125, 127, 133, 134, 161, 162, 164, 166, 167, 181
Labat, René, 36,
Lamchichi, Abderrahim, 37
Lamine, Zeroual, 21

Lamyar, 58
Larijani, Ali, 11
Laroui, Abdallah, 4
Leca, Jean, 37
Leff, 60
Lenski, Gerhard, 175
Leveau, Remy, 37
Liberia, 48
Libya, 16, 17, 28, 29, 42, 43, 57
Lidri, Houcine, 172
Lyautey (Louis Hubert Gonzalve, Marechal), 169

Ma El Ainain, 2, 58
Maazouzi, Mohamed, 37
Maghnia, 27
Maghreb ix, 4, 5, 34, 40, 41, 43, 45, 58
Makhzen, 60
Mali, 28, 31, 41, 42, 56, 57
Malta, 43
Mann, Michael, 36
Maroc x, xi, xii, 1–4, 10, 13–16, 17, 19, 21, 28–30, 32, 34, 41–43, 45, 51, 54–63, 65, 70–76, 80, 82, 83–86, 94, 107, 109, 117, 121, 125, 128, 1333, 135, 140, 142–145, 149, 152, 153, 160–163, 165–171, 173, 175–181
Marrakech, 3, 57, 110, 125, 127, 133, 134, 141, 181
Martel, Frédéric, 37
Martin A.G.P, 1, 2
Martinoli, Piero, 60
Marx, Karl, 176
Mauritanie xii, 3, 28, 30, 41, 42, 56–59, 61
Mawerdi, Aboul-Hasan Ali, 60
Mediene, Mohamed (Tewfik), 21
Mediterranean xii, 4, 28, 41, 43, 46
Melillia, 78
Menasir, 58
Mentzel, Herbert, 118
Merton, Robert King, 176
Mesaoud, Larbi, 172
Meyat, 58
Millar, John, 37
Mohammadia, 127
Mohammed V, 15
Mohammed VI, 52, 54, 55
Mohsen-Fenan Khadija, 37

Mommsen, Wolfgang Justin, 37, 78
Montagne, Robert, 60, 80
Montesquieu, C De, 9, 31, 37
Moroccan National Center for Scientific and Technical Research, 55
Moscow, 178
Moudawana, 157
Moulay, Abdelaziz, 1
Moulay, Hassan, 2
Moulay, Yacoub, 126
Mountbatten (Lord), 180
Muslim Brotherhood, 30

Nadel, Siegfried F., 79
Naïmi, Mohamed, 3, 65
National Liberation Front (FLN), 14, 22
NATO, 30, 41, 49
Nedroma, 27
Negri, Antonio, 36, 178
Nezzar, Khaled, 21
Niger, 28, 41, 42, 56, 57
Nigeria, 42
Noumria, Brahim, 172
Nun, 42

O'Donnell, Guillermo, 37
Operation Enduring Freedom Chad, 41
Oued Draa, 58
Oued Ed-Dahab, 2, 84, 85, 109, 110, 124, 125, 127–129, 132–134, 161, 163, 164, 166, 167, 171, 181
Oulad Bou Sbaa, 58
Oulad Dlim, 58, 59
Oulad Tidrarin, 58
Oulad Yahia Ben Otmane, 59
Owen, Roger, 36

Pakistan, 29
Palestine, 29
Pan Sahel Initiative, 41, 42
Parsons, Talcott, 79
Party of Justice and Development, 30
Peloponnesian Wars, 9, 31
Poles of Prussia, 78
Polisario Front, 17, 35, 45, 60, 61
Portugal, 43

Rabat, 16, 34, 74, 109, 110, 124, 125, 127, 128, 132–134, 141, 181
Rabat-Salé, 124, 125

Radcliffe, Cyril, 180
Ramdane, Abane, 21
Rapoport, Anatol, 31, 32, 35
Reagan, Ronald, 10, 35
Renan, Ernest, 69, 78
Rezette, Robert, 65
Rguibat, 57–59, 138, 141, 173
Rif saint Moulay Abdessalam Ben
    Machich, 59
Rio De Oro (Oued Ed-Dahab), 2
Romilly, Jacqueline de, 31
Rouhani, Hassan, 11
Rouquié, Alain, 37
Rousseau, Jean-Jacques, 79
Rulleau, Claudine, 37
Russia, 10, 20
Rwanda, 48

Sahara ix, x, xi, xii, 2–4, 14, 15, 22, 28,
    34, 42, 43, 55–59, 62, 70–796, 81–87,
    94, 95, 102, 104, 109, 114–117, 121, 123,
    132–135, 137–145, 148, 149, 152, 153,
    157, 161–173, 175–179, 183
Sahel, 41–46, 60
Sahrawi x, xi, 3, 4, 51, 56–59, 61, 70–78,
    81–83, 94, 19, 124, 137–143, 145, 149,
    152, 153, 171–173, 177–179
Saint Cyprian Bay, 58
Saint Simon, 37, 79
Sakia El Hamra, 3, 59, 102, 110, 133, 181
Salafia Jihadia, 44, 49
Salafist Group for Preaching and
    Combat (SGPC), 41, 42, 45
Sanhadja, 3
Saudi Arabia, 29
Schmitter Philippe, 37
Schumpeter, Joseph, 5 (Schumpeterian),
    21, 37, 176
Sebta, 78
Sedar Senghor Leopold, 47
Senegal, 42, 57
Shils, Edward, 78
Sidi Ahmed El Aroussi, 58
Simmel, Georg, 79, 149
Skocpol, Theda, 176
Smara, 2, 58, 183
Smith, Adam, 27, 37, 79
Smith, Anthony, 78
Solomon xi
Somalia, 48

Sous, 3, 56, 58
Sous-Massa, 84–86, 94, 110, 125, 128,
    133, 134, 149, 181
Soviet Union, 10, 14, 16, 20, 27, 34
Spain x, 2, 3, 11, 41, 43, 57, 78, 142
Special Operations Command Europe
    (SOCEUR), 41
Spencer Herbert, 37
Stockholm International Peace
    Research Institute, 63
Stora, Benjamin, 37
Stouffer, Samuel A., 173, 174
Stuart, James, 37
Sudan, 57, 60
Sutcliffe, Bob, 36
Sweden, 65
Syria, 11, 12, 29

Tablighis, 45
Tajakant, 58
Takna, 59
Tan Tan, 127, 142, 173
Tanger, 110, 127, 133, 134, 181
Taoubbalts, 58
Tarde, Gabriel, 105
Tarfaya, 142
Taroudant, 84, 85, 125, 126
Tazaroualat, 58
Teheran, 178
Tekna, 3, 58, 60
Tell, 59
Tetouan, 74, 133
Thomson Scientific, 55
Thucydides, 9, 31
Tiarat, 14
Tidikelt, 2, 15
Timor (East), 180
Tindouf, 15, 58, 61, 76
Tiris, 58
Tito, Josip Broz, 19
Tiznit, 58, 126, 149
Tlemcen, 16, 27
Tocqueville, Alexis de, 44, 159, 160, 173,
    180
Todd, Emmanuel, 176
Touareg, 28, 45
Touat, 1, 15
Trans-Sahara Counter-Terrorism
    Initiative, 42, 43
Trout, Jack, 37

Tucker, A.W., 32
Tunisia, 14, 15, 28, 29, 34, 42, 43
Turkey, 12, 30

U.S. State Department, 41, 63, 65
United Kingdom, 43, 63, 65
United Nations, 53, 55, 56
United Nations Security Council, 56
United States, 10, 11, 27, 35–37, 40–43,
  49, 63, 65
United States European Command
  (EUCOM), 42
USAID, 43

Villiers, Guy de, 37

Weber, Max, 26, 48, 49, 50, 69, 78, 79,
  173, 176
Weimar Republic, 26
Whitehead, Laurence, 37
World Values Survey, 52
Wright, Mills Charles, 36

Yafseh, Abdelkader, 37
Yakout, 58
Yasuda, 145
Yugoslavia, 48

Zenaga, 58
Zouerate, 61